THE POWER OF
EFFECTIVE
READING INSTRUCTION

how NEUROSCIENCE
INFORMS INSTRUCTION *across*
ALL GRADES *and* DISCIPLINES

KAREN GAZITH

Solution Tree | Press   *a division of*
Solution Tree

555 North Morton Street
Bloomington, IN 47404
800.733.6786 (toll free) / 812.336.7700
FAX: 812.336.7790

email: info@SolutionTree.com
SolutionTree.com

Visit **go.SolutionTree.com/literacy** to download the free reproducibles in this book.

Printed in the United States of America

Library of Congress Cataloging-in-Publication Data

Names: Gazith, Karen, author.

Title: The power of effective reading instruction : how neuroscience informs instruction across all grades and disciplines / Karen Gazith.

Description: Bloomington, IN : Solution Tree Press, [2023] | Includes bibliographical references and index.

Identifiers: LCCN 2023027956 (print) | LCCN 2023027957 (ebook) | ISBN 9781954631779 (paperback) | ISBN 9781954631786 (ebook)

Subjects: LCSH: Reading. | Effective teaching. | Teacher effectiveness. | Classroom environment.

Classification: LCC LB1050 .G36 2023 (print) | LCC LB1050 (ebook) | DDC 418/.4071--dc23/eng/20230814

LC record available at https://lccn.loc.gov/2023027956

LC ebook record available at https://lccn.loc.gov/2023027957

Solution Tree
Jeffrey C. Jones, CEO
Edmund M. Ackerman, President

Solution Tree Press
President and Publisher: Douglas M. Rife
Associate Publishers: Todd Brakke and Kendra Slayton
Editorial Director: Laurel Hecker
Art Director: Rian Anderson
Copy Chief: Jessi Finn
Senior Production Editor: Suzanne Kraszewski
Cover and Text Designer: Kelsey Hoover
Acquisitions Editor: Hilary Goff
Assistant Acquisitions Editor: Elijah Oates
Content Development Specialist: Amy Rubenstein
Associate Editor: Sarah Ludwig
Editorial Assistant: Anne Marie Watkins

ACKNOWLEDGMENTS

First and foremost, I thank my husband, Tsafrir, for providing guidance and insight whenever needed. In addition, I would like to thank my three children, Ben, Adam, and Adina, with special thanks to Adina for helping edit and provide suggestions throughout the writing process.

A special thank you to Solution Tree and, in particular, the editing team of Amy Rubenstein and Suzanne Kraszewski. You have been invaluable in supporting the book's vision and paying attention to every detail.

This book was a labor of love. Educating all people in a way that allows them to thrive as students and humans is a deeply held belief of mine, and this deep-seated belief has its roots in the early experiences my parents provided me. I owe my belief in inclusion and educational equity to my mother, Dena Cohen, who was an outstanding educator. Finally, my brother Robert Cohen inspired me to advocate for all people with disabilities who, more than anyone else, rely on a sound, evidence-based educational system.

Solution Tree Press would like to thank the following reviewers:

Lindsey Bingley
Literacy and Numeracy Lead
Foothills Academy
Calgary, Alberta, Canada

Doug Crowley
Assistant Principal
DeForest Area High School
DeForest, Wisconsin

John D. Ewald
Education Consultant
Frederick, Maryland

Agnes Miller
Test Coordinator and Academic Dean
Charlotte, North Carolina

Luke Spielman
Principal
Park View Middle School
Mukwonago, Wisconsin

Jennifer Steele
Assistant Director, Athletics and
Activities
Fort Smith Public Schools
Fort Smith, Arkansas

Visit **go.SolutionTree.com/literacy** to download the free reproducibles in this book.

TABLE OF CONTENTS

Reproducible pages are in italic.

CHAPTER 3

Reading and Response
to Intervention

ABOUT THE AUTHOR

Karen Gazith, PhD, is a faculty lecturer in the Department of Educational and Counselling Psychology at McGill University, where she also serves as the graduate program director for the Certificate of Inclusive Education and the education and counseling psychology liaison for the Certificate in Inclusive Education for the Office of First Nations and Inuit Education. She serves additionally as the director of the Bronfman Jewish Education Centre of Federation CJA and is also the author of *Teaching With Purpose: How to Thoughtfully Implement Evidence-Based Practices in Your Classroom*. She holds a strong belief that teachers play a critical role in the success of their students, and she has presented worldwide on topics related to developing key competencies in leadership, inclusive education, evidence-based practices, differentiated instruction, response to intervention, and assessment and instruction.

Dr. Gazith began her teaching career at the Feuerstein Institute in Jerusalem, where she implemented Dr. Feuerstein's Instrumental Enrichment Program for young children and adolescents. She has taught at Hebrew College in Boston and the University of New Brunswick. From 2018 to 2020, she served as the academic project leader for McGill University Faculty of Education's *Determining Best Practice for Students with Learning Challenges in Quebec: Comprehensive Review and Knowledge Mobilization*.

Dr. Gazith has won numerous excellence awards at Federation CJA in Montreal, including the Pearl Feintuch Award, the Gewurz Award for Jewish Educational Leadership, and Federation CJA awards of excellence. She received scholarships from Les Fonds pour la Formation de Chercheurs et l'Aide à la Recherche from the Quebec government, as well as from the Scottish Rite Foundation for doctoral research. Dr. Gazith earned a doctorate in education and counselling psychology from McGill University.

To learn more about Dr. Gazith's work, visit teachingmeanslearning.com and follow @GazithKaren on Twitter.

To book Karen Gazith for professional development, contact pd@SolutionTree.com.

INTRODUCTION

In my graduate course on the teaching of reading, I show my students a video clip from a session of the U.S. Congress in Washington D.C. (Yale Center for Dyslexia & Creativity, 2017). In the clip, a group of reading researchers and parents of students with a reading disability present the urgency for policy to guide better practice for the teaching of reading, especially for students with reading challenges. What strikes me most about the plea is the bottleneck the researchers and parents describe in the implementation of best practice learned from research in teaching reading.

Since the early 2000s, there has been an abundance of research on reading. Much of this research comes from the advent of functional magnetic resonance imaging (fMRI), which enables researchers to identify the brain areas involved in reading by observing increased blood flow in specific regions (Agarwal, Sair, Gujar, & Pillai, 2019; Brignoni-Perez, Jamal, & Eden, 2020; Nijhof & Willems, 2015). These studies shed light on how we learn to read and why some students struggle to read. As the researchers and parents presenting to Congress in the video clip reveal, little of what has been learned about reading from the research has made its way into the classroom. As the research base continues to grow, what has been learned about the brain and reading should inform reading practices in schools—not just in reading instruction, but across all content areas.

Because of the critical role that evidence-based practice plays in reading instruction in the early grades and overall effective reading instruction from elementary through high school, we must heed the call of these researchers and parents by ensuring that what we know about how students learn to read is brought into our schools. This book will highlight the neuroscience research on reading as well as evidence-based practices throughout the grade levels and across content areas so that students can become proficient readers.

The Problem

In 2017, The National Assessment of Educational Progress posited that about one-third of fourth graders in the United States have poor literacy skills and struggle to comprehend fourth-grade reading material (National Assessment of Educational Progress, 2017). Equally, if not more significant, two-thirds of the students who drop out of school have reading problems, and an even higher percentage, 85 percent, of students in the juvenile court system struggle to read (Sweet, 2004; Katiyar, 2021). The inability to develop basic proficiency in reading results in people being blocked from attaining essential information about health, diet, hygiene, and other basic needs, thus exacerbating inequality (Castles, Rastle, & Nation, 2018). According to the World Literacy Foundation (as cited by Castles et al., 2018), the lack of basic reading proficiency carries a direct cost of more than $1 trillion U.S. dollars, not to mention the many indirect costs to people's sense of self, well-being, and their overall mental health (Castles et al., 2018). Despite an abundance of research about how students learn to read and the grim consequence of not learning to read, these poor statistics have not changed since the 1980s (Kilpatrick, Joshi, & Wagner, 2019).

According to the American Psychiatric Association (APA, 2013) reading challenges are highly prevalent among students. Approximately 48 percent of Canadians (Statistics Canada, 2015) and 52 percent of Americans (National Center for Education Statistics, 2017) have low literacy skills. Moreover, about 10 percent of the population has a learning disability disorder (University College London, 2013), and about 80 percent of them are in reading (APA, 2013; Learning Disabilities Association of America, 2015; Shaywitz & Shaywitz, 2008). According to researchers, approximately 60 percent of the variation in the performance of students lies either between schools or between classrooms, with the remaining 40 percent being due to either variation associated with students themselves or to random influences (Townsend, 2007, p. 774).

According to many jurisdictions in Canada and the United States, reading is a right and not a privilege (Gewertz, 2020; Ontario Human Rights Commission, 2022). A court case in Canada, Moore v. British Columbia, reaffirms reading as a human right, stating "human rights laws in Canada protect the right of all students to an equal opportunity to learn to read" (Ontario Human Rights Commission, 2022, p. 2). In 2022, the Ontario Human Rights Commission (OHRC) engaged in a public inquiry into the right to read as well (Ontario Human Rights Commission, 2022). According to the OHRC (2022), "Literacy goes beyond the ability to read and write proficiently. It includes the ability to access, take in, analyze and communicate information in various formats, and interact with the different forms of communication and technologies" (p. 4). This commission said so articulately, "The inquiry is not just about an equal right to read—it is about an equal right to a future" (Ontario Human Rights Commission, 2022, p. 2).

Unfortunately, since the early 2000s, despite the extensive research on effective reading practice based on solid neuroscience research, there continues to be a battle about the most effective way to teach reading—what is termed the "reading wars" (Rothman, 1990). The pendulum swings back and forth between the need to use an explicit approach to teaching students sound–letter correspondence and a whole-language approach, which researchers who advocate sound–letter correspondence term "a psycholinguistic guessing game." Remnants from the past whole-language approach to reading remain in practice in some schools and districts despite the years of evidence espousing challenges with this approach (Castles et al., 2018; Moats, 2007).

Advocates of a whole-language approach believe that children need to develop a love for reading through rich literature texts and that more systematic approaches to teaching cause children to dislike reading and contribute to the difficulties they experience (Castles et al., 2018). To reach a middle ground, a balanced approach to reading was developed (Fisher, Frey, & Lapp, 2023). The belief was that students could learn phonics to a degree, but phonics should be only one method taught to students. Students should also learn to use context to make sense of the words on the page and ultimately learn to read and comprehend text. This method prompts students to look at pictures to gain meaning or guess a word from the context (Castles et al., 2018). The two largest states in the United States, California and Texas, adopted this balanced reading approach. Very soon, all states began to use this approach that was tied to a philosophy rather than based on the science of reading. Despite being termed a "balanced approach," there remained a far greater emphasis on using cues such as pictures or reading the first letter and guessing rather than a more phonics-based approach to reading (Fisher et al., 2023).

In addition, reading is often seen as just the responsibility of the language arts teacher rather than everyone's responsibility. But when students struggle with reading, they struggle with content and in all disciplines. According to Gabriella Daroczy, Magdalena Wolska, Walt Detmar Meurers, and Hans-Christoph Nuerk (2015) and Gonzalo Duque de Blas, Isabel Gómez-Veiga, and Juan García-Madruga (2021), students perform significantly worse on mathematics word problems than on similar problems written in number form. Additionally, mathematics assessments using word problems will always be an assessment of students' reading skills (Daroczy et al., 2015; Duque de Blas et al., 2021; Martiniello, 2008). Students with reading challenges continue to struggle (Aslam, 2018; Kang & Shin, 2019; Witzel & Mize, 2018). Therefore, it's vital for all teachers to learn how students learn to read and the foundational skills necessary to engage in higher-level reading skills, such as analyzing the text, so that those struggling to read will be supported throughout all content areas. To further emphasize this point, starting at around fourth grade, students need to be able to transition from learning to read, where teachers have hopefully used a phonics-based approach to ensure that students are becoming skilled decoders, to a more sophisticated ability to use these skills and then read to learn (Toste & Ciullo, 2017). Unfortunately, many students struggle when they reach the higher grades of middle and high school because of their poor mastery of the skills essential to proficient reading comprehension (Wanzek, Wexler, Vaughn, & Ciullo, 2010). It is therefore essential to ensure that students develop the essential skills required to become proficient readers (the big 5 of reading) and when students struggle to read, educators identify where the breakdown has occurred (NICHD & USDOE, 2000; Swanson, Barnes, Fall, & Roberts, 2018).

Research shows the positive impact of early identification and intervention (Dodge et al., 2015; Lovett, Frijters, Wolf, Steinbach, Sevcik, & Morris, 2017; Wanzek, Stevens, Williams, Scammacca, Vaughn, & Sargent, 2018). For example, according to the National Reading Panel (2000), "by 4th grade, 2 hours of specialized instruction is required to make the same gains that would have resulted from 30 minutes of daily instruction if begun when the child was in Kindergarten" (p. 146). Furthermore, if students are not reading at grade level by the third grade, there is a 75 percent chance that they will never read at grade level (Education Advisory Board, n.d.)—not because they are unable to learn to read, but because formal reading instruction typically ends by the end of grade two (Genlott & Grönlund, 2013; Reading Rockets, n.d.a.).

In addition, the COVID-19 pandemic presented additional challenges for students vulnerable toward a reading disorder or who had already been identified as having a reading disability (Panagouli et al., 2021; Vouglanis & Driga, 2023). COVID-19 resulted in an ever-increasing gap between students at risk for reading development and the grade-level expectations primarily because of the time spent out of school. Providing students at risk for a reading disorder with additional support in reading inoculates them against more significant risk.

The Solution

If we are to transform reading proficiency for our students, we need to focus on reading instruction in our schools and our classrooms, ensuring that evidence-based practices are applied consistently and with fidelity. The goal should be to provide all students with evidence-based reading instruction and identify those not reaching benchmarks. The way to ensure student proficiency is not to officially label all students; rather, the solution is effective instruction for all and intervention for those in need. Furthermore, reading is everyone's business. Every teacher must take it upon themselves to understand how students learn to read and how to support those who are struggling. This book begins with a chapter devoted to the research on the neuroscience of reading and how the human brain has adapted over time. Research indicates that when educators use evidence-based practices, students become more proficient readers. As Shaywitz and Shaywitz (2016) state:

> We are now in an era of evidence-based education. Objective scientific evidence—provided by brain imaging studies and the National Reading Panel's rigorous scientific review of the literature—has replaced reliance on philosophy or opinion. (p. 153)

Since the 1990s, there has been substantive research on the most effective methods that should be used to teach students to read so they will become skilled adult readers. The research has been examined in governmental reviews in the United States, the United Kingdom, Australia, and other countries, and these reviews have led to a clear consensus highlighting the importance of a phonics-based approach to reading. Despite the vast amount of research, there remains debate about the most effective approach that should be used to teach students to read. According to Castles and colleagues (2018), educators desire to hold onto whole language instruction because of the belief that phonics ignores the additional elements of reading that includes vocabulary development and comprehension of text. Therefore, this book focuses on the big 5, which highlight the importance of five reading skills: (1) phonemic awareness and (2) phonics, and also (3) vocabulary, (4) fluency, and (5) comprehension (Ontario Human Rights Commission [OHRC], 2022), leading to students becoming proficient adult readers who love to read and are able to comprehend complex texts. An abundance of evidence supports the importance of the big 5 and with it the critical role that phonics plays in early reading development (OHRC, 2022).

This book is written for educators, clinicians, and policymakers who are either directly teaching students, working with struggling students, or setting policies for literacy instruction in schools. It highlights evidence-based practices in reading across all content areas. Thus, those involved in the education of students primarily in K–8 will find many practical strategies and suggestions for improved education for elementary students highly beneficial. There is a wide range of teachers who can benefit from the content of this book; elementary through high school teachers will gain a deeper understanding of the neuroscience of reading. This knowledge allows teachers to better understand how students learn to read and why some students struggle. And perhaps most important, this book highlights strategies for teaching reading using the big 5 principles, specifically, how to help students with reading challenges. The book's final chapters discuss reading development across all content areas. In the book, I will explain how students who struggle to achieve basic reading proficiency continue to struggle as they progress into middle and high school. Effective instruction using the big 5, especially vocabulary, fluency, and comprehension, is crucial to closing the gap. Content-area strategies in the social sciences, science, and mathematics are presented so teachers can provide evidence-based support to students throughout all disciplines and grades.

About This Book

This book begins with an exploration of the most recent neuroscience research on reading development in chapter 1. Neuroscience research conducted since the 1990s has significantly enlightened the field regarding how students learn to read.

Chapter 2 addresses the big 5 of reading—(1) phonemic awareness, (2) phonics, (3) vocabulary, (4) fluency, and (5) comprehension—with an explanation of each and specific strategies that teachers can apply within the classroom.

Chapter 3 summarizes the key elements of response to intervention (RTI), a three-tiered model to support the learning of all students. In particular, the chapter highlights how, within this model, teachers screen students to ensure they are developing fundamental reading skills and how to support those who, through the use of these screening tools, show signs of difficulty with reaching specific reading benchmarks.

Chapter 4 focuses on models to support students who are slightly or more significantly off track with their reading development. Specifically, the chapter highlights acceleration, anchor activities, push-in and pull-out, and accommodation and remediation.

Chapter 5 reviews strategies to support the fundamental reading skills of decoding and fluency across all content areas. Every teacher is a reading teacher because every teacher must ensure students have the basic skills to engage with the text at increasingly higher levels of complexity. Teachers of content areas such as history and geography may not be able to teach all of the fundamental skills; however, they can at least identify when these skills interfere with student progress.

Chapter 6 addresses general strategies for strategic teaching and learning within the classroom. The chapter describes a guided approach—gradual release of responsibility—that involves naming the strategy, explaining when and why it's used, and following a modeled process of "I do, we do, you do one, and then you do many." (Pearson & Gallagher, 1983).

Each chapter concludes with a reproducible Next Steps tool you can use to examine the most important elements learned in the chapter and reflect on how the elements will influence your teaching or work with students.

The Best Way to Teach Reading

In my experience, educators are passionate about supporting students with reading development and helping them overcome the challenges they often face. My hope is that with this resource, educators will understand that all students can learn how to read if taught well—that the acquisition of language (speaking) is natural, but reading isn't—and they will be able to teach reading to all students and put into place strategies for those students struggling with reading. The best way to teach reading isn't a matter of opinion. We have research that relies on neurobiology proving what works. The abundance of research in reading that leads to models of effective reading practice and concrete strategies that can make a difference for our students must be implemented if we are to eliminate the bottleneck for the benefit of all our students.

CHAPTER 1

THE NEUROSCIENCE OF READING

Our capacity for language is evolutionarily built into our brains—a skill that's been present for thousands and thousands of years (Wolf & Gottwald, 2016). Put so articulately by Steven Pinker, "There is almost no way to prevent it from happening, short of raising a child in a barrel" (Pinker, 2009, p. 29; Castles et al., 2018). Of course, there will be variability in children's language development, but if exposed to language, they will learn to talk. When parents and other caregivers speak to a baby, the infant eventually begins to babble (Golinkoff, Can, Soderstrom, & Hirsh-Pasek, 2015), and then as the child grows, they develop the capacity to string a few words together and eventually begin speaking. Reading development, however, has a very different history than that of spoken language.

From an evolutionary perspective, reading is a relatively new invention, only around 5,000 years old (Wolf & Gottwald, 2016). Unlike speaking, reading is not natural. In essence, writing, visual symbols that represent spoken words, is a code that students need to break (Castles et al., 2018). Reading requires a rewiring of the brain; the regions initially tasked with language are now needed to turn printed words into meaning. Stanislas Dehaene and Laurent Cohen (2011) aptly call this occurrence *neuronal recycling*, and neuroplasticity makes this possible. *Neuroplasticity* refers to changes in neural circuitry, as well as synaptic connections within the brain in response to learning and the environment. The brain has the capacity to change its structure and function as a result of activity, such as going for a walk in the woods or through learning how to map letters onto their sounds (Kaczmarek, 2020). Maryanne Wolf, the author of many books on the history of reading and how the brain learns to read, states, "the human brain learned to connect some of its most basic structures and processes in new circuits that became, over only several millennia, unparalleled in their neural complexity" (Wolf & Gottwald, 2016, p. 72).

Many aspects of neuroscience could seem overwhelming to a teacher. However, considering the capacity of the brain to change itself through effective instruction, neuroscience should be relevant and exciting for teachers who are, in fact, brain changers. When we teach effectively, we create new neural connections for students that are transformative. A student who is a non-reader can transform into a reader and grow to be an avid reader. Furthermore, when students develop reading proficiency, specific parts of their brain develop advanced and proficient circuitry, operating like an efficient highway (Dehaene, 2009). One critical region of the brain I discuss in this chapter is the word form center, or the part of the brain that becomes activated when students master decoding and fluency. Once students develop proficiency at the word level, reading becomes automatic, and looking at a word and not processing it becomes impossible. To truly understand a text, students need to focus all their attention on meaning and, therefore, fluent reading plays a crucial role in proficient comprehension. It enables students to focus all their attention on the meaning of the text and not on how to read it. Therefore, all teachers should understand how students develop fluency.

The parts of the brain critical to reading development function as a circuit, with each part sharing in the responsibility, leading to proficient reading comprehension. Understanding how reading circuits function and that each step in the process is a stepping stone to the next—from the early awareness of the features of spoken language, to breaking a word into syllables and phonemes, to mapping the sounds onto letters, to mastering vocabulary, to reading with accuracy and speed—enables educators to teach students effectively and ensure mastery of this sophisticated and miraculous reading process (Wolf et al., 2016). For this system to be effective, explicit instruction is essential.

Neural Recycling and the Consolidation of Neural Networks

As researchers Dehaene and Wolf point out, the brain has an extraordinary capacity to rewire itself to adapt to new requirements, but only within limits (López-Barroso, de Schotten, Morais, Kolinsky, Braga, Guerreiro-Tauil, Dehaene, & Cohen, 2020; Wolf, Ullman-Shade, & Gottwald, 2016). Two limitations in particular warrant attention. First, despite the capacity for the brain to rewire itself and use systems that were not intended for reading to enable the individual to read, the brain centers initially tasked with a specific function need to maintain that function even when moving into a new realm, the realm of reading. For example, the visual brain responsible for identifying vision and faces must now take on new responsibilities, such as letter identification. Second, despite the sophistication of our brains and the capacity for rewiring, early language development with exposure to books is essential; therefore, children living in impoverished language environments are at a disadvantage (Wolf et al., 2016).

The areas of the brain that undergo neural recycling to make meaning of printed words are those formerly tasked with speech production and articulation and language comprehension (López-Barroso et al., 2020). Additionally, from an evolutionary perspective, our brains were wired for survival—to identify specific features in nature with the rapid speed needed to stay alive, to determine how far away an animal was or whether or not a plant was poisonous. These neural pathways had to be repurposed to recognize the fine features of letters. This region of the brain that used to process images was hijacked to eventually process words quickly and efficiently (Krafnick, Tan, Flowers, Luetje, Napoliello, Siok, et al., 2016). Many reading tasks are processed within 300 to 500 milliseconds (Wolf & Gottwald, 2016).

The three primary regions that have had to be repurposed for reading are the visual centers in the occipital, temporal region at the back of the brain, language areas in the parietal-temporal region of the midbrain, and speech pronunciation, language, executive, and motor regions in the frontal part of the brain (see figure 1.1, page 12). In particular, the visual processing network in the posterior region and the language networks in the anterior and midbrain regions need to reorganize themselves to develop the capacity to see a word, analyze the sounds, decode it by mapping each letter onto the sound it represents, and eventually commit it to visual memory for increase efficiency. This brain reorganization is needed because our brains need to recognize that words are made up of sounds that have a written counterpart. Eventually, the sounds are connected to the letters they represent and read quickly and with ease (Wolf & Gottwald, 2016).

As students learn to read, they need to gradually consolidate the visual and language networks into one that enables the reader to become proficient at reading sophisticated text with ease and comprehension. But for young readers, these networks are not yet consolidated. Thus, the reading process is more belabored and requires a lot of mental effort (Dehaene-Lambertz, Monzalvo, & Dehaene, 2018). Initially, students activate the parietal-temporal region to decode words—letter by letter, which is an arduous process. However, with ongoing practice, the occipitotemporal area

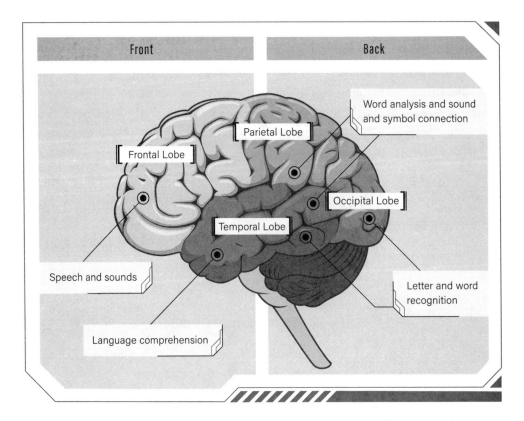

FIGURE 1.1: Regions of the left hemisphere of the brain that have had to be repurposed for reading.

becomes activated, resulting in automatic reading (Pugh, Mencl, Jenner, Katz, Frost, Lee et al., 2001; Church, Coalson, Lugar, Petersen, & Schlaggar, 2008; Ben-Shachar, Dougherty, Deutsch, & Wandell, 2011).

So, before becoming readers, young children use visual and language regions of the brain to process what they will later learn are words. This happens because they are not yet decoding but becoming familiar with commonly seen visuals, such as *McDonald's*, *Cheerios*, and other words they regularly see. *Decoding* refers to the student's ability to map each phoneme, such as /b/, /d/, /g/, and /ph/, onto the letter or grapheme (letter combination such as *ph*) that represents that sound. When students are decoding, they are reading each word based on the letter; this is sound knowledge. This is contrasted with the ineffective practice of students who look at a whole word and guess what it says based on information such as the visual shape of the letter or using other cues such as a picture associated with a word. Phillip E. Gough and William E. Tunmer (1986) refer to *decoding* as "[context-free] word recognition" (p. 7) contingent on knowledge of the letter-sound correspondence rules.

However, this stage of early reading is essential because, even though students have not yet learned to decode, they are becoming aware that there is a word form that can symbolically represent a concept.

As students become early readers, the parietal-temporal lobe of the left hemisphere assumes the task of early reading development (Sprenger, 2013). The left hemisphere, in the mid and back regions, is activated as the child learns to phonologically parse words into their component sounds because this task requires the left brain's analytic capacity. Interestingly, this circuitry is specific to reading alphabetic languages such as English, French, and German. In logographic languages such as Chinese and Japanese Kanji script, activation in proficient readers can be seen in both the left and right hemispheres of the occipital and temporal regions (Kim & Cao, 2022). This is particularly interesting as it indicates the critical role of the occipital and parietal areas of the left hemisphere in alphabetic languages to break up sounds into their parts—and map the sounds on the specific letters they represent. As you'll see later in this chapter, struggling readers resemble early readers in terms of a lack of activation in the left hemisphere; instead, the activation occurs in both the right and left hemispheres when attempting to read (Sprenger, 2013).

As Stanislas Dehaene (2009) aptly notes:

> Every child is unique . . . but when it comes to reading, all have roughly the same brain that imposes the same constraints and the same learning sequence. Thus, we cannot avoid carefully examining the conclusions—not prescriptions—that cognitive neuroscience can bring to the field of education. (p. 449)

Despite what the neuroscience says about how students learn to read, some educators continue to argue for a mixed instruction model of reading instruction that applies whole language and phonics instruction in the classroom. The use of these two methods of instruction is based primarily on the faulty belief that there are unique differences among learners; thus, students benefit from being taught to read using the method that addresses their individual needs (Spiro & Myers, 1984). In fact, an abundance of research since the 1990s shows that students need to use the phonics route to decode so they can map the sounds of language onto the letters they represent. Once they decode the word, they can access its meaning and eventually read sentences, paragraphs, and texts (Goswami & Bryant, 2016).

Development of Speed and Efficiency

When a child learns to read, precise and pronounced changes occur in the brain's higher-order visual regions that enable the brain to respond to written text. Additionally, associations are established between auditory and speech areas in the brain and higher-order visual regions, enabling students to respond quickly and effortlessly to written language (Dehaene, Cohen, Morais, & Kolinsky, 2015).

This reading process requires enormous speed and efficiency. When information enters the system, it first goes to the thalamus, which can be likened to the brain's relay center, sending the word to the visual cortex of the occipital lobe, which has to visually process or make sense of these squiggly and straight lines. The parietal-temporal region, toward the mid and back of the brain, breaks words into parts or sounds, and once the reader has learned to do this, the occipital-temporal lobe at the back of the brain kicks into action. The occipitotemporal lobe is responsible for assimilating the orthography and the phonology of the word, or the way it looks and sounds (Shaywitz, Shaywitz, & Shaywitz, 2021). Figure 1.2 shows the thalamus as part of the reading systems (Sprenger, 2013).

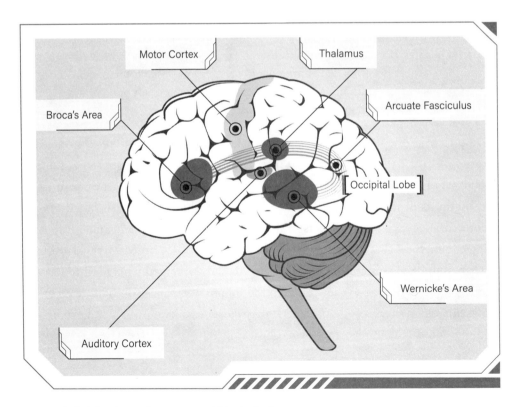

FIGURE 1.2: The reading process within the brain.

The reader will eventually need to develop a network of neurons stored in this occipital region, creating an automatic visual representation of the word. This process is essential for reading fluency and comprehension because to understand what is being read, the reader needs to read quickly and with ease. The occipital brain region lets the reader identify words without slowly sounding out each letter. In other words, the reading process must become automatic. Changes occur in the brain as readers increase in proficiency. Early readers show greater activation in the left parietal-temporal region of the brain, which is the region that analyzes the word and breaks it into parts or sounds (Chyl et al., 2023). However, studies conducted on the brain's reading process of proficient readers show the greatest activation in the word form area, indicating that they are no longer decoding but can now read quickly and easily, a process that eludes poor readers.

Research has been conducted to examine the factors enabling this efficiency. In particular, researchers have investigated the role of white- and gray-matter pathways, which support the efficiency of this process. Gray matter is the tissue in the brain's outermost layer, getting its grayish color from the high levels of neuronal cell bodies, and its role is to process information in the brain. Studies examining the relationship between gray matter volume in specific regions of the left hemisphere and reading find that increased gray matter is associated with higher levels of reading proficiency, and those with dyslexia (also discussed in the following section) show lower gray matter cortical volume in critical left hemisphere regions (Church et al., 2008; Linkersdörfer et al., 2015; Williams, Juranek, Cirino, & Fletcher, 2018).

According to Jason Yeatman, Robert Dougherty, Michal Ben-Shachar, and Brian Wandell (2012), white matter enables effective communication among critical brain regions and facilitates the myelination process, gradually increasing speed and efficiency in addition to pruning unnecessary axons. This pruning process is crucial because it frees space for further myelination of axons in areas essential for the reading process. Ultimately, white matter links the visual and the language centers, so language to print is processed quickly and efficiently. Furthermore, research indicates that the level of white and gray matter in infants and early readers is predictive of reading in kindergarten—and this is highly important as a potential marker of reading challenges (Zuk et al., 2021). Finally, Nadine Gaab likens this process to an efficient highway because well-developed highways allow cars to move quickly and easily—and a high level of speed and efficiency is required for the complex skill of reading (Reading Rockets, 2019).

There may appear to be a contradiction here. Are students' reading brains unique or not? Let's return to Dehaene's quote on page 13 to answer this question. Of course, children are unique, but when it comes to the reading brain, the same constraints and requirements are needed for individuals to become proficient readers. This is not to say that every reading brain looks the same. For example, individuals with reduced gray and white matter might have lower efficiency, but to go from a non-reader to a reader, the same neural connections must be established in the brain.

When Reading Is a Challenge

Unfortunately, the cultural invention of reading is a skill that poses a significant challenge for approximately 10 percent of the population who have dyslexia (Al-Shidhani & Arora, 2012). Dyslexia is a neurobiological disorder that was first identified by Adolph Kussmaul, a German professor of medicine, and labeled *dyslexia* shortly after by ophthalmologist Rudolf Berlin (Kirby, 2020). Also known for his early work on this disorder, a physician named Pringle Morgan published a report about a fourteen-year-old boy who was "intelligent" but could not read. A few years later, Hinshelwood described another case of a ten-year-old child described as bright who struggled to read. Hinshelwood noted that "the difficulty in learning to read was due not to any lowering of the visual acuity, but to some congenital deficiency of the visual memory for words" (Hinshelwood, 1900, p. 1507, as cited in Kirby, 2020).

However, from the early 1890s until the 1980s, most of the research on dyslexia was based on reading characteristics of students who struggled to make sense of the printed word. Starting in the 1980s with positron emission tomography (PET) and then fMRI in the 1990s, what had been a hidden disability was now receiving greater prominence for its neurological correlates (Demb, Boynton, & Heeger, 1998).

Bennett Shaywitz and Sally Shaywitz (2020) conducted a critical study using fMRI in 2002, where they studied 144 students, half of whom were diagnosed with dyslexia and half of whom were typical readers. This research and other studies that followed found less activation in the posterior regions of the left hemisphere in students diagnosed with dyslexia.

An important question for researchers was whether these regions show underactivation because these individuals struggle to read or if there are early brain markers of underactivation in these critical areas even before individuals with dyslexia learn to read. Research on prereaders with a family history of dyslexia shows underactivation in these key posterior reading areas (Raschle, Zuk, & Gaab, 2012). Individuals with dyslexia typically take in the same information as their age cohorts, but their ability to process written language is impaired. Regions in the left hemisphere, such as the parietal-temporal area tasked with word analysis, decoding mapping letters onto their corresponding sounds, and the occipital lobe that is charged with quick access to words leading to fluency, show reduced activity. Also, dyslexic readers don't show the same left-hemisphere asymmetry when attempting to read (Shaywitz & Shaywitz, 2020).

fMRI research into dyslexia has also provided insights into which parts of the brain activate during different reading tasks through the examination of increased blood flow to these specific regions (Agarwal et al., 2019; Brignoni-Perez et al., 2020; Nijhof & Willems, 2015). From this, researchers have identified the particular location and activity associated with a task—such as single-word reading. The advent of fMRI technology advanced the field because it does not require invasive radioactive materials, which were part of the early functional research using PET scans (International Dyslexia Association, 2020).

Therefore, fMRI technology can be used with students and adults, allowing for longitudinal research designs that can be used to increase our understanding of dyslexia (International Dyslexia Association, 2020). As indicated above, fMRI research studies have shown that individuals with dyslexia show underactivation in three regions of the left hemisphere, namely the parietotemporal region, the frontal region, specifically the inferior frontal gyrus, and the occipitotemporal region, including the visual word form area responsible for rapid word recognition. Important to note here is that current research focusing on examining whole-brain connectivity finds increased connectivity in the right hemisphere and reduced connectivity in the visual word form area (Finn et al., 2014). Importantly, PET scan research and fMRI show that individuals with dyslexia have a unique neural signature leading to poor reading; they are not lazy or lacking effort (Shaywitz & Shaywitz, 2020).

Additionally, research into the differences in structural features of the brain in individuals with dyslexia show reduced gray and white matter in these specific regions (Rahul & Ponniah, 2021). Gray matter, mainly composed of nerve cells, is found on the outer portion of the brain and is responsible for processing information. As mentioned, white matter can be found deeper in the brain regions and is mainly responsible for supporting the communication between nerve cells. Reduced gray matter in these essential regions may impact the students with dyslexia's ability to process individual language sounds. The reduced white matter may impact the overall efficiency of reading.

More nascent research using functional magnetic spectroscopy (MRS), which measures neurometabolites, examines the role of specific neurotransmitters, specifically choline and glutamate, on reading challenges. Researchers have found that individuals with dyslexia have an increased level of these chemicals, impacting white matter organization and creating hyperexcitability. These atypically developing neurocircuits may explain the difficulties processing information, which is essential for reading and makes it more difficult for students to consolidate new learning. This heightened level of certain chemicals creates a lack of stability in the way in which students respond to reading requirements, or their reaction times. For example, it may take them longer to respond to a prompt such as, What are the sounds you hear in the word *dog*? Or, Read this word: *dog*. According to Hornickel & Kraus, (2013), students with dyslexia show greater "moment-to-moment variance," thus impacting their reading development.

From an educational perspective, teachers need to view reading challenges as an actual disorder rather than some behavioral trait of students who lack motivation or desire to read. Yes, students who struggle to read may eventually lose their motivation. However, motivation or other behavioral traits are the response to their atypical processing rather than a cause for poor reading. Dyslexia, or its new term, *specific learning disability in the area of reading*, continues to be challenged as a legitimate disorder affecting many students and adults (APA, 2013). Journalists such as Julian Elliott and Elena Grigorenko, Rod Little, and Peter Hitchens have challenged this in their harsh critique of the disorder. They claim that "'dyslexia' is useful only to parents seeking to excuse their students' difficulties and 'should be consigned to the history books'" (Kirby, 2020, p. 473). For too many years, the common belief was that students with dyslexia had low I.Q.s and weren't smart, and this faulty belief led to torment for students with dyslexia and their families (Shaywitz & Shaywitz, 2020). Thankfully, research has led to enlightenment about what dyslexia is—and what it isn't.

Thanks to the brain's malleability and knowledge of effective practice from research, students who struggle to read can develop into more efficient readers. Even after a few hours of use, research-backed strategies, such as GraphoGames, you begin to see changes in the brain—neuroplasticity in action. Shaywitz and Shaywitz's (2020) research on the structural changes in the brain is essential to developing hope in students with dyslexia and their parents and teachers. Through effective evidence-based practice, teachers are changing students' brains to enable them to transition from being nonreaders to becoming readers.

According to Shaywitz and Shaywitz (2020), it is now possible and relatively easy to screen for dyslexia early on, even as early as kindergarten, before formal reading instruction has begun. This means that intervention can begin even before a student realizes that they are unable to do something their classmates are doing. For example, preschool and kindergarten teachers can assess children's phonological awareness skills, assessing their ability to recognize and generate rhymes, segment compound words into two separate words, segment words into syllables, and segment phonemes in a word, and the ability to identify the sounds associated with letters.

From Non-Readers to Readers

Explicit teaching that includes phonics rules and how language is structured is essential. All students need to understand the relationship between sounds and letters. For the reasons explained in this chapter, this process eludes many students. Once they understand the relationship between sounds and letters, they then need to develop increased efficiency and reading fluency by activating the word form center. As mentioned in chapter 1, the word form center, located in the occipitotemporal region of the brain, is critical for rapid word recognition. The ultimate desired process for students to acquire, of course, is to derive meaning from text. Teachers need to learn how to teach this modern cultural invention of reading to all students so that every student can be successful in school and in life, and benefit from the joys of reading.

Conclusion

The next chapter explores the big 5 of reading—(1) phonemic awareness, (2) phonics, (3) vocabulary, (4) fluency, and (5) comprehension—identified by the National Institute of Child Health and Human Development (NICHD) and the U.S. Department of Education (USDOE; 2000), providing the research base followed by specific strategies for teaching each in the classroom.

The Neuroscience of Reading: Next Steps

The most important elements I learned about the neuroscience of reading	How this element will influence my teaching or my work with students	Reflections

CHAPTER 2

THE BIG 5 OF LITERACY

In 1997, the U.S. Congress charged the National Institute of Child and Health Development to work with the U.S Department of Education to establish a reading panel tasked with identifying research on the best, most effective ways to teach students how to read (NICHD & USDOE, 2000). The fourteen-member panel made up of educators, school administrators, and reading scientists reviewed over 100,000 research studies on how children learn to read to determine the most effective, evidence-based methods and practices and find ways to share this information with school systems throughout the United States. The panel concluded their work on April 13, 2000 (NICHD & USDOE, 2000), finding that all literacy instruction must include five essential areas of reading development: (1) phonemic awareness, (2) phonics, (3) vocabulary, (4) fluency, and (5) comprehension, which have become known as *the big 5 of reading*.

This chapter explains each of the big 5 areas of reading development in detail and provides strategies to teach each one. To become proficient readers, students must master all five elements of literacy, so it is imperative that each of these elements be taught explicitly. But before we begin a discussion of the big 5, it is critical to bring awareness to the importance of early reading.

The Importance of Early Reading

There is extensive evidence that print awareness and understanding how print is organized on a page is an essential early reading skill (Justice & Sofka, 2010). Students who have limited exposure to print may come to school with limited experience with how print is organized on the page and how books are structured (Treiman, Rosales, & Kessler, 2016).

For example, children need to know that a title page provides information about the book and contains the story's title and author's name. Also, they must learn that we read text from top to bottom, and we start on the left side and read to the right, then return sweep, meaning we continue on the left side of the following line. When we complete one page, we move to the next page. These elements of print awareness are essential foundational features of texts. If children are not exposed to print early before starting school, they may be at a disadvantage when they attempt to learn to read.

Print awareness comes from ongoing exposures to print in storybooks within a child's environment. To enhance print awareness in the home and the classroom, children should be read to daily; in classrooms, there should be print on walls around the school, and teachers should point out words and read them aloud, indicating that words are made up of individual sounds. The early literacy classroom can put all students in good stead on the road to reading when teachers emphasize and teach these skills daily (Treiman et al., 2016). In preschool and kindergarten, teaching phonemic awareness should be the focus. However, it is essential for students to get early exposure to books and words in order to gain a strong foundation for phonemic awareness.

The Big 5

Students depend on effective reading instruction that incorporates the big 5 of literacy—phonemic awareness, phonics, vocabulary, fluency, and comprehension— into all aspects of reading. Each one of these skills depends on the effective mastery of the preceding skill. For example, to develop effective letter-sound mapping skills, students need to have mastered the awareness that words are made up of sounds that can be manipulated. To become fluent readers, students need to master phonics—the ability to decode words by mapping each sound in the word onto the letter representing that sound. Vocabulary development is essential to develop proficient comprehension. And, most important, comprehension of text depends on the effective mastery of each of the previous four building blocks. Consequently, mastery of the big 5 is essential if students are to become proficient readers and explicit teaching is needed to ensure student mastery. Students who do not master basic reading skills by grade 3 are at significant risk of failing to succeed in school; explicitly teaching the big 5 and ensuring mastery can drastically improve the lives of students.

We will begin with the first of the big 5: phonemic awareness.

Phonemic Awareness

Phonemic awareness is the ability to process the individual sounds in spoken language (Gillon, 2018), and blend, segment, and manipulate each of the individual sounds of a word. Phonemic awareness forms the foundation of students' eventual reading ability.

Phonemes

All words are made up of phonemes. A *phoneme* is the smallest part of language—otherwise referred to as a *sound particle*. In the English language, there are more than forty phonemes with corresponding sounds (see table 2.1, page 24), including consonants, diagraphs, short vowels, long vowels, and controlled vowels. For example, a phoneme could be the sounds /p/, /b/, /sh/, or /ch/.

To understand the concept of a phoneme, it's important to understand phonological awareness. *Phonological awareness* refers to the sound pattern of language and is an essential skill for later reading development. Phonological awareness starts to develop in infancy.

As mentioned in the previous chapter, during early language development, infants hear the language spoken to them. Adults are preprogrammed to use a high pitch when speaking to infants and a cadence separating speech sounds (Narayan & McDermott, 2016). For example, a parent might say to an infant or small child, "Mo-mmeeee is here," using a slow pace and pronouncing each sound. The young child eventually begins to babble, and this reciprocal relationship between the adult and child's communication is essential to the eventual language production (Fusaroli, Weed, Fein, & Naigles, 2019).

As the child develops and continues to hear spoken language, they start to recognize that language has a pattern and can be broken into unique parts. The first and perhaps easiest pattern for them to recognize is that some words have similar ending sounds, referred to as rhymes. The awareness of rhymes typically develops at four to five years of age (Dessemontet, de Chambrier, Martinet, Moser, & Bayer, 2017). When reading a rhyming book to a young child, the child's laughter each time a rhyming word is read signifies that the child is developing phonological awareness—or awareness of the language pattern. According to many reading researchers, the child's ability to recognize and later generate rhymes is the best early indicator that the child is developing phonological awareness (Grofčíková & Máčajová, 2021; Jing, Vermeire, Mangino, & Reuterskiöld, 2019).

TABLE 2.1: List of Phonemes, Spelling, and Examples

	PHONEME	SPELLING (INITIAL POSITION)	SPELLING (FINAL POSITION)	EXAMPLE
Consonants				
1	/p/	p	p	*pick, hop*
2	/b/	b	b	*bid, knob*
3	/t/	t	t, bt, ed	*tap, doubt, flipped*
4	/d/	d	d	*deck, bad*
5	/k/	k, ch, ck	k, ch, ck	*can't, kick, rook, lock*
6	/g/	g, gu, gh	g, gue, gg	*give, guitar, ghost, bag, plague, egg*
7	/m/	m	m, mb, mn	*map, jam, limb, hymn*
8	/n/	n, kn, gn	n, gn	*neck, knick, sign, pen, gnat*
9	/ng/	–	ng	*sing*
10	/f/	f, ph	f, ff, ph, gh	*fate, photo, leaf, off, graph, enough*
11	/v/	v	ve	*vote, give*
12	/s/	s, c, ps	ce, se, ss, s	*sick, mice, center, base, psychology, bliss, bus*
13	/z/	z	se, ze, zz, s, z	*zap, please, sneeze, buzz, has, whiz*
14	/j/	j, g	ge, dge	*juice, giant, guage, dodge*
15	/y/	y	–	*yell*
16	/hw/	wh	–	*what*
17	/w/	w	–	*warm*
18	/h/	h, wh	–	*house, who*
19	/l/	l	ll	*look, fell*
20	/r/	r, wr	r	*rake, far, wrong*
Digraphs				
21	/sh/	sh, s	sh	*shoe, rash, sure*
22	/ch/	ch	ch	*chick, batch*
23	/zh/	si, s, z	–	*vision, treasure, azure*
24	/th/ (unvoiced)	th	th	*thank, thong*
25	/th/ (voiced)	th	th	*feather*

	PHONEME	SPELLING (INITIAL POSITION)	SPELLING (FINAL POSITION)	EXAMPLE
Short Vowels				
26	/a/	a, a_e		sat, have
27	/e/	e, ea, ai, a		pet, head, said, many
28	/i/	i, y, e, I_e, ee, ui		six, gym, pretty, give, been, build
29	/o/	o, a		log, watch
30	/u/	u, o, o_e, ou		but, ton, love, young
31	/oo/	oo		book
Long Vowels				
32	/a-/	a_e, ai, ay, ea, ei, ey, eigh		late, bait, say, steak, veil, they, sleigh
33	/e-/	ee, ee, ea, y, ie, e_e, ey, i_e, ei		me, feet, bead, many, field, these, key, machine, receive
34	/i-/	i_e, y, i, ie, igh, ye		time, try, mild, pie, high, lye
35	/o-/	o, o_e, oa, ow, oe, ou, ew		so, hope, coat, low, toe, soul, sew
36	/u/	oo		loon, moon, noon, soon, spoon
37	/y/ /u/	y, u, ew, iew, eau, ieu, eu, u_e, ueue		you, uniform, few, view, beauty, adieu, feud, yule, queue
38	/oi/, /oy/	oi, oy		boil, toy
39	/ou/, /ow/	ou, ow		cloud, now
Controlled vowels				
40	/a/	air, are, ear, ere, eir, ayer		chair, square, pear, where, their, prayer
41	/ur/	ur, ir, er, or		turn, girl, her, work
42	/o/	aw, a, or, oor, ore, oar		paw, ball, fork, door, more, board
43	/ea/	ear, eer, ere, ier		ear, steer, here, pier
44	/ua/	ure, our		cure, tourist
45	/aw/	aw, au, a(l), a(ll), ou		saw, cause, walk, ball, cough

Sources: Dyslexia Reading Well, n.d.; Literacy Connects, n.d.

The next step in the progression toward phonological awareness is the child's ability to break words into isolated syllables, which typically develops around four to five years of age as well (Gillon, 2018). As you may notice, as a child progresses toward phonological awareness, the sound pattern or particle gets smaller and more challenging to process. An example of syllabication is e/le/phant or bi/cy/cle.

The next skill children develop in the phonological awareness trajectory is the ability to segment words by onset and rimes (not to be confused with rhymes). For example, in the word *flash*, the onset is the beginning consonants—/fl/—and the rime is the vowel and remaining consonant—/ash/. At approximately six years of age, children should be able to break words into onset and rime (Gillon, 2018).

The most challenging skill in the phonological awareness trajectory is phonemic awareness: the ability to break words into individual sounds (Gillon, 2018). This skill typically begins with the child isolating the first sound in a word, such as the /c/ in *cat*, then the last sound, such as the /t/. The middle sound is typically the most difficult to identify (Catts, 1995, as cited in Hougen, 2016).

Also, part of phonemic awareness is the ability to blend individual phonemes or sounds of a word. For example, after hearing the sounds /c/, /a/, /t/, the child needs to blend the sounds to form the word *cat*. This skill develops around six years of age (Gillon, 2018). Segmenting words into phonemes is more complex and involves the ability to hear the word *cat* and segment it into phonemes such as /c/ /a/ /t/.

The last step in the trajectory is the ability to manipulate phonemes (Reid, 2016). For example, the child would be able to utter the word *cat* without the /c/, forming the word *at* or replacing the sound /c/ with another sound, such as /f/ to create the word *fat*.

Phonemic Awareness and Reading Development

The NICHD and USDOE (2000) reading panel found that early training in phonemic awareness skills, especially blending and segmenting phonemes, substantially benefits reading acquisition. Also, the committee found evidence that phonemic awareness should be taught directly and implicitly. In other words, educators and parents should constantly help students break words into parts, either through formal activities or informal means.

Phonemic awareness is essential to reading development because to read, students need to have mastered the ability to hear each sound in a word and eventually map each sound onto a letter. Researchers have found that "even though comprehension is the hallmark of skilled reading, it is not comprehension per se that presents the major hurdle for the most struggling young readers" (Hempenstall, 2013, p. 10). Most reading problems observed in students occur primarily at the level of single-word decoding (Hempenstall, 2013). In most cases, the difficulty with phonemic awareness reflects an underlying struggle with some aspect of phonological awareness. (Milankov, Golubović, Krstić, & Golubović, 2021). Therefore, early childhood education must highlight phonological awareness skills as part of the curriculum.

Furthermore, students with reading problems have also been shown to have phonologically based difficulties (Milankov et al., 2021). If you can't process the sound /c/ in *cat*, it will be impossible to map the sound onto the written word *cat*. Students who struggle with phonemic awareness (the ability to process individual sounds in a spoken word) typically hear only the entire word being uttered. For example, when asked to isolate the individual sounds in *cat*, they would likely say *cat*. If you can't isolate individual sounds in a word, such as the /c/ in *cat*, it will be impossible to map the /c/ sound onto the letter c. Therefore, phonemic awareness must be taught and learned.

Finally, English has an irregular orthography, meaning there are many possible phonemes for each sound in the English written language (Marinelli, Romani, Burani, & Zoccolotti, 2015). A perfect 1:1 ratio exists when each letter of the alphabet makes one sound. To illustrate this point with just a few examples, the phoneme /i/ can represent many different sounds, such as the i in words like *pint* and *mint*, the s in *is* or *island*, or the gh sound in *cough* and *bough*.

Exercises for Phonemic Awareness

As soon as children begin preschool, they should be learning about phonemic awareness through games and other fun and enjoyable activities as a constant focus of their time in school. Every time they leave the classroom, teachers should ask them to tell us the sounds they hear in simple words (for example, "What are the sounds you hear in /c/ /a/ /t/?), increasing the difficulty throughout the year (such as, "If I remove the /c/ from the word *cat*, what new word do I have?"). Teachers should also read books with rhyming and alliteration and stop throughout the reading to ask questions such as, "What other word begins with the sound /b/?"

As mentioned, explicit teaching of phonemes is essential. Still, for young children, early exposure to sounds should begin with a focus on the larger umbrella of phonological awareness. For example, identifying and then generating rhymes (*cat* and *bat*), segmenting sentences into words ("I am eating an apple."), segmenting compound words into single words (*sunshine* becomes *sun* and *shine*), segmenting words by syllables (a-ni-mal), and segmenting words into onset and rimes (f/ish) are all essential skills to master.

In preschool and kindergarten, phonemic awareness should be taught in earnest, with a block of time each day devoted to the explicit teaching of phonemes and how words are made up of these individual phonemes or sounds. However, some children struggle to master phonemic awareness skills before entering first grade.

Teachers should use consonant-vowel-consonant (CVC) words such as *cat*, *bat*, *kit*, *fit*, and *jam* because these are the easiest words to blend and segment (Ehri, 2022). When teaching children individual phonemes—for example, the first sound they hear in the word *rat*—it is essential that teachers avoid including what's termed a *shwa*—or the /uh/ sound after pronouncing the /r/ phoneme. Including the /uh, for example, ruh for the sound /r/ in *rat*, will make it impossible to segment or blend the sounds in a word. For example, *rat* will be pronounced as /ruh/-/a/-/tah/.

The question arises, *Should phonemic awareness continue to be taught to children in grade 1 and beyond?*—and the answer to this question is tricky. Given the importance of phonemic awareness to the mastery of phonics, children who have not yet acquired mastery—meaning that they are not yet able to efficiently and consistently blend, segment, and manipulate phonemes—should continue to receive targeted support in grade 1. However, learning phonemic awareness beyond a basic level does not lead to more proficient advanced skills such as fluency (Reading & Van Deuren, 2007). Some research has shown that beyond kindergarten, decoding skills are far more predictive of reading success than phonemic awareness (Al Otaiba, Kosanovich, Torgesen, Kanhi, & Catts, 2012). There is little evidence that advanced phonemic awareness benefits reading proficiency. This is important as many programs have emerged that espouse the benefit of advanced phonemic instruction, such as orally segmenting multisyllabic words, such as *bringing* or *Saturn*. The problem is that, given the limited amount of time for reading instruction, phonemic awareness is replacing phonics instruction—an essential building block for proficient reading fluency and comprehension. The large amount of class time spent on phonemic awareness activities in grade 1 and beyond represents grave missed opportunities for students, especially those at risk for developing reading difficulties, because not enough time is devoted to decoding and mapping sounds onto letters (Clemens et al., 2021).

The following strategies are recommended exercises to teach phonemic awareness.

Using Sounds to Teach Phonemes

In this exercise, students learn to isolate phonemes by connecting each phoneme to a sound. The teacher uses objects that make sounds, such as a tambourine and a bell, and clapping and snapping sounds. The teacher first presents three sounds, one after the other, and asks students to identify each sound. For example, the teacher could ring a bell, crumple paper, and bang on the wall. The students would then need to state each sound. The teacher then pairs each sound with a phoneme. For example, the teacher might ring a bell and say /b/, crumple paper and say /a/, and then bang on the wall and say /t/. Students then identify each phoneme they heard without mentioning the environmental sound, just the phoneme.

Isolating Phonemes

In this exercise, students learn to count the number of phonemes they hear in each word. Developmentally, children typically hear the first sound, then the last sound, and finally the middle or medial sound. Teachers can use this activity throughout the day—upon entering the class in the morning, when leaving for recess, or at the end of the day, students could be asked to isolate the phonemes in a word. Each time students respond, teachers document (mentally or in writing) if students are mastering the skill. Figure 2.1 shows a chart to keep track of student mastery. A zero indicates the skill has not yet been mastered, one indicates students are in the process of getting it, and two shows they have learned it. With preschool and kindergarten students, when students demonstrate mastery, they can be challenged with more difficult phonemic awareness tasks (such as deleting phonemes by showing images and having students practice saying the word without the first sound [*hat* without the *h*]) as the teacher continues to work on basic phonemic awareness skills such as phonemic segmentation with those who have not yet shown consistent mastery. Teachers provide students who have mastered the skill with another activity they can work on independently.

	Skills		
Student	Segmenting phonemes	Blending phonemes	Manipulating phonemes
Rebecca	1	1	0
Sam	2	2	2
Claudia	1	1	2
David	1	0	0

FIGURE 2.1: Student mastery chart.

Using Elkonin Boxes

Elkonin boxes are a great activity to help students identify phonemes. Students use a paper with three squares drawn on it (Toy Theater, n.d.). The teacher says a CVC word, for example, *bin*, and the students place a poker chip in a box for each sound they hear. Figure 2.2 shows an example of an Elkonin box used to identify phonemes.

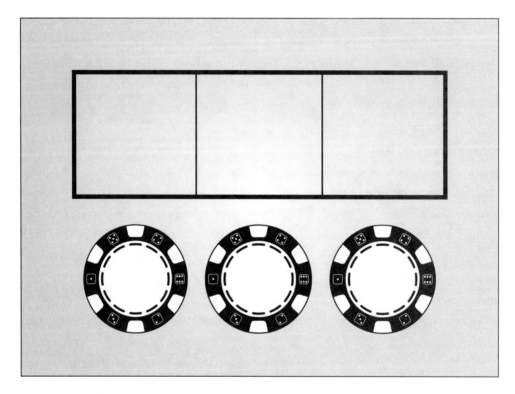

FIGURE 2.2: Example of an Elkonin box.

Blending and Segmenting Phonemes

Since phonemic awareness involves the segmenting and blending of phonemes, it is beneficial to students if teachers devote time to modeling how to segment words into individual phonemes or sounds. Teachers start by isolating the first sound in the word, for example, by asking students what the first sound is they hear in *cat*, *mat*, or *fin*. Each student segments a word into phonemes independently. For example, the teacher would provide each student with a different word and ask them to identify the first sound they hear in the word. Subsequently, students could get a lot of practice by segmenting words into individual phonemes throughout the day. Teachers should note students who are having greater difficulty segmenting and blending words into phonemes; these students will need additional support during the day.

Phoneme Manipulation

Slightly more challenging is *phonemic manipulation*, or the ability to remove or replace phonemes in a word. For example, a teacher could ask, "What word would I have if I replaced the sound b in *bat* with a c?" (*cat*), or "If I removed the sound b from *ball*, what word would you have? (*all*)." Teachers use basic CVC words for this strategy, like *mop* ("What word would you have if you replaced the m in *mop* with a b (*bop*)? These CVC words can be real words or pseudowords.

Phonics

Phonics is an evidence-based instructional approach to teaching reading that focuses on the relationship between the letter or grapheme and the sound that each grapheme represents (McArthur et al., 2018).

Sound–Symbol Association

To read, students need to develop alphabetic insight—the knowledge that each grapheme in a word represents a single sound. In other words, to read the word *dog*, students need to learn that each of the three graphemes in this word represents individual and specific sounds that must be decoded. When students are decoding words, they sound out each grapheme to accurately read the word. The goal of phonics instruction is to teach students that letters represent sounds of spoken language and that there is a predictable way to decode words. At first, decoding should follow a predictable pattern using primarily CVC words such as *dog* and *cat*. Later, typically in third grade and once students have learned the predictable pattern of decoding words and have developed alphabetic insight (each grapheme represents a single sound), students should be exposed to words that don't follow this simple pattern, such as the words *bough*, *cough*, and *bought*.

Unfortunately, despite the amount of data indicating the importance of accurate word reading, debate continues about the most effective way to teach students how to read (Muijs & Reynolds, 2018). Most students who are poor readers have difficulty associating individual graphemes or letters with the sounds they represent, and the explicit teaching of this correspondence is critical to proficient reading (Sayeski, Earle, Eslinger, & Whitenton, 2017). As with phonemic awareness, phonics should be taught explicitly and systematically rather than by presenting whole words or words for which students have not yet learned the associated sounds (the whole language approach). With effective instruction, most students will master phonics. Importantly, teaching students to guess at sounds is the antithesis of effective phonics instruction because the only way to become an effective reader is to learn the sound–symbol association between each grapheme and the sound that it makes. Students need to know that there is a one-to-one correspondence between the grapheme and the associated sound. Therefore, phonics instruction must be systematic and explicit. This sound–symbol association can be transparent, meaning that most letters represent one associated sound (as in Hebrew and Arabic), or opaque, where letters or letter patterns can represent multiple sounds (as in English). Some languages, such as Italian, Spanish, French, and Finnish, are somewhere between opaque and transparent (Ijalba & Obler, 2015). It's important to note that learning to read in one language facilitates decoding in a second or third language.

According to researchers Moniek Schaars, Eliane Segers, and Ludo Verhoeven (2017), students who have mastered the concept of grapheme–sound association in kindergarten will have a smoother transition to reading instruction in grade 1. Most kindergarten students are not yet expected to be able to decode, but they should recognize letters found in familiar words, such as the first letter in their name. Therefore, it's important for kindergarten teachers to introduce each letter, one at a time, and associate each letter with the sound it represents by using pictures that embed the sound (for example, a picture of a mountain, which embeds the /m/ sound in the letter m, or a baseball bat, which embeds the /b/ sound in both *bat* and *baseball*).

Phonics and Reading Development

The National Reading Panel's work finds that systematic and explicit teaching of phonics improves early reading ability and ultimately impacts students' reading comprehension skills (NICHD & USDOE, 2000). The panel also finds that early phonics instruction is critical for students at risk of developing reading problems. Douglas Fisher, Nancy Frey, Dominique Smith, and John Hattie (2021) further find a .54 effect size when students are taught explicit phonics. Other meta-analyses have strongly advocated for explicit phonics instruction (NICHD & USDOE, 2000; Dessemontet, Martinet, de Chambrier, Martini-Willemin, & Audrin, 2019).

Phonics instruction must eventually lead to the student's ability to sound out each grapheme in written language. This process will ultimately become automatic, leading to students becoming fluent readers, thus facilitating the ability to comprehend text (Ehri, 2015). The Primary National Strategy (2006) finds that students who don't learn according to phonics rules but instead use alternative methods to learn how to read unknown words "later find themselves stranded when texts become more demanding and meanings less predictable" (p. 10).

Strategies for Phonics Instruction

Unfortunately, despite all the evidence on the importance of explicit and systematic instruction, many schools continue to use reading programs that do not follow a systematic phonics approach to reading instruction (Bowers, 2020). Literacy instruction, and especially the teaching of phonics, should be sequential and follow a logical pattern of instruction. Therefore, it's essential for schools to have a scope and sequence of reading instruction at each grade level so that earlier skills help to develop more complex skills.

Systematic Phonics Instruction

In systematic phonics instruction, words that are easier to read, such as CVC words, are taught before more challenging words, such as consonant-vowel-consonant words that end in *e* (CVCE words) like *bake*.

In grade 1, students should learn to decode most CVC words and decode two-syllable words that follow basic patterns, such as *hello* or *cabin*. Also, beginning in grade 1, students should learn to read words with common rimes such as -at, -an, -ap, -it, -in, -ip, and so on (see table 2.2). The teaching of rimes is fundamental because it exemplifies reading patterns. The learning of rimes should continue into grade 2.

TABLE 2.2: List of the Most Common Rimes and Examples

RIME	EXAMPLES	RIME	EXAMPLES
-ack	*back, black, crack, jack*	-ide	*bride, glide, hide, pride*
-ail	*jail, mail, pail*	-ight	*bright, fight, night, right*
-ain	*gain, grain, main, pain*	-ill	*bill, chill, dill, drill, fill*
-ake	*cake, flake, lake*	-in	*grin, pin, sin, spin, thin*
-ale	*bale, gale, male, pale, sale*	-ine	*nine, pine, shine, spine*
-ame	*blame, came, dame, flame*	-ing	*cling, king, ping, ring, sling, wing*
-an	*bran, can, an, man*	-ink	*blink, drink, ink, kink, link, shrink, wink*
-ank	*bank, blank, crank, frank, rank*	-ip	*chip, clip, dip, drip, flip, grip, hip, nip*

continued →

RIME	EXAMPLES	RIME	EXAMPLES
-ap	*cap, clap, gap, tap, scrap*	-it	*bit, fit, lit, mit, pit, quit, wit*
-are	*care, date, fare, glare, pare*	-ob	*cob, job, knob, mob, sob*
-ash	*dash, flash, gash, mash*	-ock	*block, dock, flock, knock, shock*
-at	*cat, fat, hat, mat, pat, rat*	-oke	*broke, choke, joke, poke, smoke, awoke*
-ate	*gate, hate, late, mate, plate*	-op	*chop, drop, flop, mop, pop, prop, stop*
-ay	*bay, clay, day, gray*	-ore	*fore, more, score, sore, store, tore, wore*
-eat	*heat, meat, neat, wheat*	-ot	*blot, cot, got, hot, knot, lot, plot, rot, shot, trot*
-ell	*bell, fell, sell, smell, tell, well*	-ug	*bug, drug, hug, jug, mug, rug, snug*
-est	*guest, nest, pest, rest, test*	-ump	*bump, hump, jump, lump, pump, stump*
-ice	*dice, lice, nice, price, rice*	-unk	*bunk, chunk, drunk, hunk, sunk*
-ick	*kick, lick, stick, thick, trick*		

Source: Dwyer, 2001.

In grade 2, students should continue to work on decoding two-syllable words with two vowels and learn common prefixes and suffixes. They should also learn irregular words found in common grade 2 level texts, such as *people, who, whose, should,* and *why* (Reading Rockets, n.d.b.).

In grade 3, students should continue to learn to decode most multisyllabic words such as *began, tiger, contain, hotel, broken, symbol,* and *costume* and grade-level irregular words such as *ankle, write, know,* and *flight.* Students should also learn common orthographic patterns such as the silent e or the double vowel rule. Some tricks accompany these rules, such as "When you stand alone, you feel weak, and it's hard to say your name (for example, the /a/ sound in *rat*), but when a friend comes along, you feel stronger and can say your name (for example, the /a/ sound in *hail*)." Students should then be presented with other irregular words such as *could, done, friend, some,* and *would,* and teachers should ensure that students have a lot of practice learning these irregular words.

By the end of grade 3, students should be decoding most words so that the focus can move to fluency, a skill essential for proficient reading comprehension (Reading Rockets, n.d.b.).

Typically, new letter sounds should be introduced every two to three days. No doubt this will differ depending on the student, but sounds should be mastered and applied with accuracy when reading words before students move on to subsequent sound–letter correspondence.

Overall, phonics instruction should follow a systematic order. A sequence presented by Read Naturally (Read Naturally, n.d.), an evidence-based reading program, suggests the following: First, students should learn CVC words or consonant and short vowel words. Second, teachers should introduce digraphs and other blends. Third, teachers should teach long vowel sounds such as final *e* or two-vowel pairs. Teachers should then introduce other vowel patterns, such as *said*. Next, instruction should focus on syllable patterns and prefixes and suffixes added to root words such as *unhappy* and *running*.

Systematic Letter Sound Instruction

There are a few considerations when deciding on the sequence of letter sounds taught to students. First, continuous letter sounds such as /m/ are easier to learn than sounds like /b/, which are discontinuous (Earle & Sayeski, 2017). Therefore, continuous sounds should be taught first. Second, sounds used to form many words should be introduced so students can form multiple words within two to three weeks of reading instruction (Earle & Sayeski, 2017). Third, a few consonants should be taught and then a vowel so that students can create words as quickly as possible. Finally, regular words should be taught before irregular words so that students will recognize the predictability of reading (even though this is often not the case in more opaque written languages) (Earle & Sayeski, 2017).

Table 2.3 shows one effective sequence to teach letter sounds.

TABLE 2.3: Effective Sequence to Teach Letter Sounds

First set	s, m, a, t
Second set	f, r, i, p
Third set	c, b, o, g
Fourth set	h, j, u, l
Fifth set	d, w, e, n
Sixth set	k, q, v, x, y, z
Seventh set	ai, j, oa, ie, ee, or
Eight set	z, w, ng, v, oo
Ninth set	y, x, ch, sh, th
Tenth set	qu, ou, oi, ue, er, ar

Source: NSW Department of Education and Training, 2009.

Some reading programs include digraphs such as /th/ and /ch/ because these will encourage reading many words. However, as indicated in the reading sequence, students should first be taught individual sounds forming common CVC words. Digraphs such as /th/ or /wh/, diphthongs such as /oo/ and /oi/, and blends such as /bl/ and /str/ should be introduced after students are decoding CVC words (Earle & Sayeski, 2017).

It's essential to begin with synthetic phonics to introduce students to letter sounds before reading books. Synthetic phonics refers to explicitly teaching the sound associated with each grapheme. Once the student has learned the grapheme used to represent the sound, they are presented with words with that grapheme. This method is slightly advantageous over analytic phonics, where they look at words such as *bug*, *rug*, and *mug* that change sounds as you change the initial grapheme and direct students to create new words with these sounds (Torgerson, Brooks, Gascoine, & Higgins, 2019).

Effective Programs to Teach Phonics

There are many evidence-based phonics programs, and it is beneficial to teachers to use any of these. For example, Itchy's alphabet (n.d.) can be used as a program for all students and a remedial program for struggling students. This program involves connecting each grapheme to a sound through images. As previously mentioned, the image is embedded in the sound so that students can learn the sound of the grapheme through the image. For example, the grapheme /b/ is embedded in an image of a bat. The sound /m/ is embedded in a picture of a mountain. These images support the learning of grapheme–sound correspondence.

Another effective, evidence-based program is Jolly phonics (Moodie-Reid, 2016). A similar approach is taken to teach grapheme–sound correspondence, but physical movements are used in addition to visual supports. For example, the student would form the grapheme with their bodies for the sound /j/.

Because of the importance of phonics instruction to students' eventual ability to decode, read fluently, and comprehend what they are reading, schools and teachers should use evidence-based sequential programs rather than isolated sheets found on teacher websites. Some worksheets focus on word sight-reading, a process to be avoided. Some of these worksheets may not necessarily be evidence-based. There are some words that students should learn to read by sight, such as the words that are commonly found in text but are difficult to decode because they don't follow the common CVC pattern, such as the words *and* and *the*. The most effective approach is to use a reading program that is evidence-based and will teach students how to decode using a sequential and logical approach.

Vocabulary

The next of the big 5 is vocabulary, which refers to the words known and used in language, including reading and producing texts (Vocabulary, n.d.). Vocabulary is essential to comprehension because if you don't know most words in a text, it is difficult to understand what you are reading (Ibrahim, Sarudin, & Muhamad, 2016), which is vital for full, rich text comprehension.

Types of Vocabulary

There are four substates of vocabulary:

1. Expressive

2. Receptive

3. Morphemic

4. Contextual

Expressive refers to the ability to speak clearly to express thoughts and ideas; *receptive* is the ability to understand spoken or text-based language (Kwok, Brown, Smyth, & Cardy, 2015); *morphemic* refers to the knowledge of word parts—individual elements that make up words, such as prefixes, suffixes, and root words; and finally, *contextual* knowledge refers to the ability to use context to make sense of language (Helman, Calhoon, & Kern, 2015). Over the years, grammar has been overemphasized and often taught in a decontextualized way—that is, grammar rules are taught independent of the context in which these rules need to be applied. Context is essential for meaning, and imbuing in students the importance of context is why grammar should be taught. For example, if you're asking a waiter for the menu, you're speaking in the present tense, or when you're asking someone to go to the movies, you're speaking in the future tense. However, vocabulary often takes a backseat to grammar. An excellent quote by David Wilkins (1972) is, "Without grammar, very little can be conveyed; without vocabulary, nothing can be conveyed" (pp. 111–112).

Additionally, researcher H. G. Widdowson (1989) states, "The more one considers the matter, the more reasonable it seems to suppose that lexis is where we need to start. The syntax needs to be put to the service of words and not the other way round" (as cited in Lewis, 2002, p. 115). Therefore, vocabulary instruction is essential to the ability to speak coherently and understand and write text.

Vocabulary and Reading Development

Even though language is natural, and we need only to be exposed to language to speak, vocabulary must be taught explicitly for students to develop a more sophisticated ability to express thoughts and feelings clearly and express themselves in writing and understand written text (Baumann, Edwards, Boland, Olejnik, & Kame'enui, 2003). According to Andrew Biemiller and Catherine Boote (2006), students will remember only 20–25 percent of the words learned indirectly but up to 40 percent of those explicitly explained. Additionally, for a new word to become part of the students' repertoire, there needs to be 16 exposures to the word—or, said differently, the student needs to use the word 16 times in varied contexts (Riccomini, Smith, Hughes, & Fries, 2015).

A sophisticated vocabulary is essential to excel in school because it is fundamental to reading comprehension across academic disciplines, such as for the ability to understand instructions, do mathematics problems, and understand questions. Therefore, if vocabulary is not explicitly taught as soon as students begin formal schooling, the words they need to understand texts will elude them. This problem will become exponential as the vocabulary used in books increases in complexity, as do the concepts students are expected to understand (Allington, McCuiston, & Billen, 2015). Additionally, words used in books are significantly different from words used in informal conversation, television programs, and language students are exposed to on social media.

Finally, according to many researchers, students need to know at least 95 percent to 98 percent of words in a written text to understand the text (Schmitt, Jiang, & Grabe, 2011).

Strategies for Vocabulary Instruction

When presenting workshops on the big 5, particularly when discussing language acquisition, I have heard teachers state that students should be able to use context to understand unfamiliar words. However, it is challenging, if not impossible, to take advantage of context if there are too many unfamiliar words. Anita Archer (2016) presents an excellent example of this. She offers this short text to exemplify this point: "Paula put down her pirn, wrapped herself in a paduasoy, and entered puerperium" (Archer, 2016, as cited in Morgan, 2016). Even though a reader may know words such as *put*, *down*, *wrapped*, and *entered*, there are too many keywords in this text that would likely be unfamiliar. Therefore, if I asked you questions such as *Where was Paula going?*, *Was she nervous?*, or *Why did she need to put down her pirn?*, you would likely be unable to respond. However, if I explicitly taught you keywords such as *pirn*, *paduasoy*, and *puerperium* before reading the text, you would be able to understand the text and respond to the questions. I would need to explicitly teach you that a *pirn* is a tool for weaving, a *paduasoy* is a Japanese-style silken robe, and *puerperium* is the time of beginning labor until birth. These words are unfamiliar to many adults, just like words that appear in grade-level texts may be unfamiliar to students. As this example illustrates, it is impossible to use context unless you know enough words in the passage (Archer, 2016, as cited in Morgan, 2016).

Explicit teaching of new vocabulary should involve: (1) An introduction to the word with a clear and concise definition, (2) a thorough description using multiple contexts, and (3) a presentation of hyponyms and collocations.

Introduction and Definition

A teacher could begin by introducing the word using images to enrich students' understanding of it. For example, for the word *trestle*, the teacher could present multiple pictures of a trestle (supporting a bridge, a table, and a stool), indicating the various uses of a trestle. When explicitly teaching new words, teachers should avoid asking students what they think the word means before they've learned its accurate meaning. The result will be a lot of shared incorrect information about the new word. Therefore, definitions of new terms should come from a reliable source, such as the teacher. Additionally, asking students to look up new words in the dictionary could be ineffective, especially for students who struggle with language. Rather than motivate students to learn new words, this could have the opposite effect, discouraging the students who are struggling.

Thorough Description

Next, teachers should provide a thorough description of the new word. They could also provide a template (for example, a Frayer diagram; Frayer, Frederick, & Klausmeier, 1969) for students to examine the word in depth. If asking students to define the word *trestle* ("a trestle is a support structure that is often used to support a bridge"), put the word in the sentence ("trestles are often used to support bridges . . . "), and give examples of what the word is ("a structure to support a flat structure") and what it isn't ("a bridge"). See figure 2.3 (page 40).

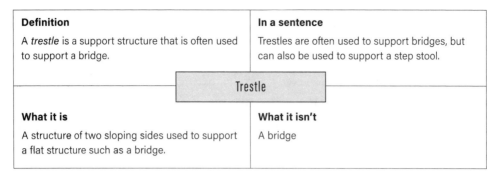

Definition	In a sentence
A *trestle* is a support structure that is often used to support a bridge.	Trestles are often used to support bridges, but can also be used to support a step stool.

Trestle

What it is	What it isn't
A structure of two sloping sides used to support a flat structure such as a bridge.	A bridge

FIGURE 2.3: Frayer diagram to teach new words.

Hyponyms and Collocations

Finally, teachers should present students with hyponyms and collocations to expand their vocabulary. A *hyponym* is a substate of a larger category. For example, a rose is a hyponym for flower, and a dog is a hyponym for animal. Presenting students with hyponyms increases their background knowledge of the words. Students could act out the new word or freeze their bodies as a physical representation of the word. Students should also be taught *collocations* or words and concepts that are often associated with the word. For example, thorns, bees, scent, pressed, artificial, and bouquet are collocations of flowers. Students will have the ability to define a word and correctly use it in multiple contexts when they have learned the word well (Moghadam, Zainal, & Ghaderpour, 2012).

It is beneficial for students to learn new words each day using this explicit format. If students learn only one new word a day, they have at least 180 new words at the end of the year. The words should be grade-level vocabulary and words students are often exposed to in grade-level texts. At least sixteen exposures to the word will ensure students are mastering it. One strategy for word exposure is to provide each student with sixteen index cards with the same word written on each card. The students wear a lanyard with all sixteen cards. Each time the student uses the word, they remove one index card. Another strategy to encourage students to use the new word multiple times during the day is to write the word on a paper wristband as a reminder to use the word.

Tier One, Two, and Three Words

Anita Archer and Charles Hughes, authors of *Explicit Instruction: Effective and Efficient Teaching* (2011), categorize words into three groups: tier one, tier two, and tier three.

- Tier one words are essential words that students are likely to pick up through casual conversation.

- Tier two words are high-frequency academic words such as *absurd* and *facilitate*. Archer and Hughes (2011) refer to these as *mortar words* because they can be used across multiple academic contexts.

- Tier three words are low-frequency words specific to a particular domain, such as *tundra*, *isotope*, and *lava*. These words are referred to as *brick words* because they are fundamental to communicating or understanding a specific subject area.

Teachers need to be especially mindful of tier two and tier three words. They should teach tier two words daily using the explicit vocabulary instruction approach. Tier three words allow students to master discipline-specific texts.

Teachers in each discipline could develop the essential tier three vocabulary they will explicitly teach to students. Table 2.4 provides some examples of words in the three vocabulary tiers.

TABLE 2.4: The Three Vocabulary Tiers

THE THREE VOCABULARY TIERS	EXPLANATION	EXAMPLES
Tier 1	Essential, common words that do not require direct instruction and words that students are likely to pick up through casual conversations. Additionally, these words do not have multiple meanings.	*girl, happy, school, building, dog, visit*
Tier 2	Common academic words that are used across multiple contexts. These words often require direct instruction.	*absurd, facilitate, compare, associate, transmit, define, express, expand, determine, analyze*
Tier 3	Uncommon words specific to a discipline or subject area requiring direct instruction.	*tundra, isotope, figurative language, hyponym, hypernym, denominator, mitosis*

Vocabulary Games

There are vocabulary games that teachers can regularly use to infuse rich vocabulary into all classroom lessons. One example Anita Archer and Charles Hughes (2011) present is the synonym race game. Students have thirty seconds to think of as many words as possible for a commonly used term like *look*, *said*, or *happy*. Classroom word walls provide students with many words from which to choose. Another game to practice vocabulary asks students to work in pairs. One partner takes a noun card such as *park* or *tiger* and has a certain amount of time to describe the noun to their partner. Students then use as many descriptive words as possible to express their words without naming the word.

Word bags is another game. Students write down the new words they learned that day during each lesson. Then, at the end of the lesson, students write these new words on paper strips (one per strip) and put them in a word bag. The following day, the teacher chooses a word from the word bag, and students write sentences with the word. Students can also write adjectives for noun words in the word bag that collocate with the noun (Watkins, 2013). Given the importance of morphemic knowledge in successful vocabulary development, teachers should teach students common prefixes, suffixes, and root words. Finally, students could rewrite a text by replacing the adjectives, nouns, or verbs. Table 2.5 summarizes these vocabulary games.

Fluency

Fluency is the ability to read with ease and accuracy to focus your attention on the meaning of the text (Rasinski, Rupley, Pagie, & Nichols, 2016). Poor readers need to exert so much effort decoding individual words that little effort remains for text comprehension (Rasinski et al., 2016). In addition, students with poor word recognition have difficulty comprehending text because previous words read fade from memory before they recognize words that come later (Rasinski et al., 2016).

Reading Quickly, Correctly, and With Expression

Speed, accuracy, and prosody or expression are factors contributing to fluency. *Speed* refers to how quickly you can read a text. To read quickly, students need to be able to decode text with ease. *Accuracy* refers to reading words correctly, and *prosody* refers to the stress or emphasis placed on words and sentences, intonation, pauses, and overall rhythm of reading. It is essential to note that fluency does not only mean reading quickly but rather reading correctly and with expression. To increase fluency, some teachers introduce sight words. However, sight words should only be used for the high-frequency, difficult-to-decode words such as *and* and *the*, because they don't follow the typical CVC pattern. Students need to learn to decode words, and emphasizing sight word reading is harmful to learners because they believe that reading is about visually recognizing the pattern of a word rather than decoding each sound. However, teaching a few common and difficult to decode words may help to increase fluency.

TABLE 2.5: Vocabulary Games

VOCABULARY GAME	EXPLANATION	EXAMPLE
Synonym Race	Students have thirty seconds to think of as many words as possible for a commonly used word like *look*, *said*, or *happy*. Display synonyms of words on the wall after students have generated their synonyms.	"Write down as many words as you can think of for the word *and*." Once students complete the task, the teacher adds the synonyms for *and* on the word wall such as *additional*, *in addition*, *also*, *as well as*, *moreover*.
Describe the Noun	Working in pairs, one student takes a noun card and has a certain amount of time to describe the word to the partner. The describer should use as many descriptive words as possible.	"*Park* is the noun card. The describer has sixty seconds to describe the word so the partner can identify the noun. The describer can say things like—'Lots of children play here, there is a slide, swings, and monkey bars, and you can have a picnic here.'"
Word Bags	Students write down new words learned during a lesson. At the end of the lesson, students write these new words on paper strips (one word per strip) and put them in a word bag. The following day, the teacher chooses a word from the word bag, and students write sentences with the word or adjectives for the word.	The teacher completed a lesson on animal habitats. During the lesson students learned new words such as *environment*, *organisms*, *niche*, *characteristics*, and *reproduction*. At the end of the lesson, students write these words on strips of paper and place them in a word bag. The following day, the teacher takes one word out of the word bag, such as *organism*, and the students write a sentence with that word. For example, Organisms need certain conditions to survive.
Rewrite the Text	Students rewrite a text by replacing the adjectives, nouns, or verbs in the text.	"Yesterday, on my way to work I saw a *friendly* dog that *ran* to me and began to lick my arm." "Yesterday, on my way to work, I saw an *affable* dog that *rushed* to me and began to lick my arm."

For students to understand text when working within an instructional context of the classroom, 90 to 94 percent of the words need to be read correctly. However, when reading independently, students need to read between 95 percent to 100 percent of the words correctly to comprehend the text. Students who read with less than 90 percent accuracy are at a frustration level and are not enjoying reading or gaining from it.

It is encouraging to see increased recognition of the increase in fluency practice. Still, many schools continue to use ineffective methods that are not evidence-based such as round-robin and extended silent reading time (Smith & Williams, 2020). According to Jan Hasbrouck (2006), these practices might have taken hold during the 1990s when researchers such as Marilyn Jager Adams (1990) wrote a synthesis of reading research, writing that for students to read well, we need to find a way to get them to read a lot. Unfortunately, despite the lack of research supporting these methods, many educators adopted strategies such as Drop Everything and Read (DEAR) and uninterrupted sustained silent reading (USSR). Osborn and Lehr (2003) state that there is a small or no gain in reading achievement from silent reading practice. A critical point to mention here is that round-robin reading, a practice common in the past that remains in practice, does not increase reading fluency. This is primarily because students are only reading a few sentences at a time and only once. Furthermore, students who are poor readers fear reading aloud and thus can't perform well because of the pressure to read aloud in front of all their classmates. Many students remember the trauma of round-robin reading and recall that because they were so full of panic, they counted the lines to find the line they'd be reading, trying to read it multiple times (ineffectively) because they were so fearful.

Fluency and Reading Development

The National Reading Panel's report highlighted the importance of fluency and the relationship between fluency and comprehension (NICHD & USDOE, 2000). Yet 40 percent of fourth graders read at a low fluency level, and research shows that they read only one- or two-word phrases without fully recognizing the sentence or its structure. This is essential for teachers to understand because fluency (speed, accuracy, and prosody) is often not given the time and attention required as a pathway toward enabling students to become proficient at reading comprehension. Problems with fluency interfere with reading comprehension because readers need to decode and construct meaning from the written word to read proficiently. These two cognitive processes are essential to comprehension, which is the ultimate goal of reading. However, the cognitive resources available for these two processes are limited in our memory capacity, and if one of these tasks, such as decoding, requires too much cognitive resource, it will inevitably limit the ability to maximize the other task, comprehension. Slow, effortful decoding or choppy reading will slow down the reading process and consume valuable resources that need to be used to make sense of the text. Furthermore, if a student incorrectly decodes many words, it will be impossible to make sense of the text. Therefore, without fluent reading, all the student's energy will need to go toward the individual word rather than on the meaning of the text. This is not conducive to understanding text. Because fluent readers do not need to focus on the individual word when reading, all of their energy is devoted to meaning, such as the author's message, why the author has chosen to write the text, and the connections between this text and the reader's own life, current affairs, or other texts read. Fluent readers can take full advantage of their background knowledge to appreciate the text.

Students must first master decoding before gaining full benefit from fluency reading strategies. This doesn't mean that students cannot practice fluency until they have perfected sound–letter correspondence, but they need to be able to decode a segment of text before moving into fluency.

Fluency is the bridge between decoding and comprehension. Therefore, to comprehend text, students need to become fluent readers.

Strategies for Increasing Fluency

Repeated oral reading is an evidence-based approach that significantly impacts reading fluency (Lee & Yoon, 2017). This approach involves students doing multiple readings of a short passage until they attain an identified fluency level. As I address in chapter 3 (page 63), fluency looks somewhat different for students struggling to read, but in this section, I address fluency practice as an effective approach for students who are meeting reading milestones and require fluency practice as a step in the process of becoming proficient readers.

It is essential to encourage students to read out of class, and silent reading is necessary during students' free time. However, class time is limited and precious. Thus, most in-class reading time should involve direct student instruction (Stockard, Wood, Coughlin, & Rasplica Khoury, 2018).

Students in younger grades could practice fluency based on the words they have successfully decoded. Still, it is important to start daily fluency practice using grade-level texts as an everyday activity in grade 3. This includes teacher modeling proficient reading because students need to hear good examples of reading proficiency. Thus, teachers could, at times, read aloud to students, emphasizing fluency instead of choppy word-by-word reading, proper pausing at commas, stopping at periods, and reading with appropriate expression. Students then partner up and read a passage using a repeated reading approach. Again, for this section, I explain the process for students reaching benchmark-level expectations. In the next chapter, I'll focus on fluency for students with reading challenges.

Teachers begin by presenting a grade-level text to all students, reading the passage aloud, emphasizing appropriate speed, word accuracy, and cadence. Students use a repeated reading process as follows until students are reading a text at their appropriate reading level, meaning no more than 5 percent errors in word accuracy. Jan Hasbrouck and Gerald Tindal (2017) researched oral fluency and developed their most recent fluency norms. Teachers could use these norms to identify if students are practicing their reading using the appropriate text. For example, according to these norms, in grade 6, to read at the 50th percentile, students should read 132 words per minute on a grade 6-level text. If they are reading at this level, they should probably continue reading this grade-level text until they are solidly at the 75th percentile. However, if students read around 90 words per minute, indicating they are at the 10th percentile, they should be given a lower-grade text to practice fluency. In short, teachers would assess student reading level and provide the text at the student's current reading level. Once students are reading proficiently at that level (regardless of their actual grade), they should progress to the next grade level.

As they progress using this strategy, teachers will likely need to differentiate students' texts by reading level as their progress level will vary.

The process is as follows:

1. The teachers assign reading partners. At first, all students should be reading the same grade-level text (for example, grade 3 level text for grade 3 students). Each student has their own file folder with the text and a chart to mark their progress.

2. Teachers ask students to identify as partner A or B and then set the timer to sixty seconds. Partner A reads the passage until the timer goes off and then draws a line after the last word read. Partner A then reads the same passage at sixty seconds following the same process another four times, totaling five times reading the passage. Each time, partner A draws a line after the last word is read. Partner A then completes the chart indicating how many words are read per minute. Partner B, who is listening to the text being read, may be able to tell how many words were read incorrectly to get a somewhat accurate count of correct words per minute. However, during the fluency practice, the goal is to read the same text five times. The exact count of words correct per minute is less critical. The teacher will call over students each week to get an accurate word count and then identify when and if students need a more or less challenging text.

3. Partner B now follows the same process—reading the passage while partner A marks the incorrect words. Again, the exact number of words correct is not important; don't worry if not all incorrect words are identified. The goal is practice using level-appropriate text.

When the teacher evaluates each student's reading fluency every week, students read a different passage but at the same grade level while the teacher determines the number of words read correctly per minute. If the student exceeds that grade-level benchmark, the student receives a more challenging text. Provide an easier text if the student is not reading according to the grade-level standard. For example, a grade 3 student who does not reach the benchmark could get a grade 2-level text. The partners would remain, even though each has a different grade-level text.

Comprehension

Comprehension refers to making meaning from text and connecting what is read to background knowledge. Durkin (1993) refers to comprehension as the "essence of reading" (NICHD & USDOE, 2000). According to the National Reading Panel, comprehension is a multifaceted process. Additionally, according to the panel, "meaning resides in the intentional problem-solving thinking processes of the reader that occur during an interchange with text" (NICHD & USDOE, 2000, p. 4–5).

Construction of Understanding

Meaning requires the deliberate construction of understanding by the reader, which requires a reciprocal interaction between the reader and the text (NICHD & USDOE, 2000). When working with students, I often ask them to imagine the author of the text sitting on their shoulder with them asking the author questions about the text. It is this active reciprocal process that is at the heart of reading. It is joyful to see readers immersed in the text—in the complete flow of learning; unfortunately, this eludes struggling readers. However, with skillful, strategic teaching, students can learn how to understand what they read.

Highly proficient comprehenders use various techniques and align their methods with the type of text they're reading, such as narrative or expository. Additionally, proficient comprehenders use metacognitive strategies and are aware of their thinking processes while reading. They also need to make deliberate decisions about what methods to use. Therefore, for successful comprehension, learners need to be taught a range of strategies that they can use for different purposes. Proficient readers understand text structure, use metacognitive strategies when reading, and recognize when texts are complex and when a specific strategy needs to be employed to make sense of the challenging text. Proficient readers know which comprehension strategy to use, successfully apply strategies to comprehend text, and often attribute their success to the strategy they used.

The use of strategies is self-motivating because it results in understanding what you're reading. Additionally, students can put forward effort when reading because they see that effort leads them to success. Thus, proficient comprehenders receive intrinsic motivation from using effective strategies. As you'll see in chapter 3 (page 63), this is a great challenge for readers who struggle.

Comprehension and Reading Development

Far too often, comprehension instruction takes the form of having students respond to questions. However, this is an assessment, not an instructional approach. Comprehension must be taught and learned using an explicit approach: Through gradual release of responsibility, the teacher guides students, modeling how strategies are applied by explicitly teaching the steps necessary. This chapter presents many strategies for enhancing students' comprehension skills. Every strategy has a set of steps to be followed.

Gradual release of responsibility is a highly effective approach to teaching strategies is to use an explicit-modeled approach of I do; we do, you do one, you do many (Rupley, Blair, & Nichols, 2009). To begin, the teacher models the process on the board, speaking aloud while reviewing each step using a grade-level text (I do). At this point, students have their full attention focused on the teacher. Next, in the we-do stage, the teacher presents another similar short text, but this time, the teacher and all the students, in unison, use the steps to apply the strategy. In the you-do-one stage, each student works independently on another similar short text. Finally, in the you-do-many stage, students complete a few examples independently. The students who continue to have difficulty would work with the teacher to review the strategy again until the students can master it.

Comprehension is the ultimate goal of reading, and with the use of diverse and varied strategies and an explicit approach that transitions from being teacher-directed to student-directed, students can become proficient comprehenders and will read to learn and for pleasure. However, to achieve this, teachers need to know a repertoire of comprehension strategies and how to teach them to their students. The extent to which students use these strategies depends mainly on the effectiveness of instruction.

Strategies for Teaching Comprehension

Comprehension strategies should be an essential part of literacy instruction even before a child can read. The most effective strategies to teach comprehension are using background knowledge, shrinking the paragraph, highlighting text patterns, reciprocal teaching, and Adler's (1940) close reading. Students should learn to use different reading methods and develop flexibility in shifting from one strategy to another depending on the situation. However, the most important factor is for students to be actively engaged when reading.

Teachers of young students could read to them and talk aloud as they apply effective strategies and engage students in active discussion about the text. For example, kindergarten teachers can use the strategies described in the preceding paragraph. As students become increasingly proficient readers, they should be able to apply these strategies when they read independently.

It is essential to name each strategy when instructing students. For example, when teaching the first strategy, applying background knowledge, the teacher would inform students that they are about to learn a new strategy. The teacher then names the strategy and tells the students that they're going to learn how to apply this effective strategy that will help them understand what they read. Teachers often teach techniques without naming them as a strategy. When this is done, students don't know that they are learning a tool that they should consistently use when presented with a new text.

Using Background Knowledge

The most powerful early indication of a three- or four-year-old child's comprehension skills is their ability to apply their background knowledge when being read to. Reading is essentially constructing meaning from text, yet to do this, the reader must know something about the text being read. A hallmark study on reading conducted in the 1980s presented participants with a text about cricket, but before asking the participants to read the text, the researchers spoke to them about baseball and made comparisons between baseball (something readers knew a lot about) and the game of cricket (a game about which they knew very little; Hayes & Tierney, 1980). Using students' background knowledge of a topic similar to the one they are about to read is an effective strategy because it links their knowledge of a familiar subject to a mostly unknown one.

Within the classroom context, teachers could facilitate a discussion about the text that students are about to read. Triggering background knowledge before reading a text is essential. Teachers can model how students ask themselves questions about the text, such as, "How much do I know about this topic? Have I read anything like this topic in the past? Where can I go to get more information on this topic?" To follow the modeled approach, teachers begin by naming the strategy: "I will teach you a strategy called *using background knowledge*," and then follow the explicit teaching approach I do, we do, you do one, and then you do many (see table 2.6).

TABLE 2.6: Using the Background Knowledge Strategy Using I Do, We Do, You Do One, You Do Many

EXPLICIT TEACHING STEP	EXAMPLE
I do: The teacher asks students to close computers, put down writing utensils, and give their undivided attention to the teacher.	Teacher: "First, I look at the title to see if I know about this topic." "Then, I look at the cover, table of contents, headings, and images and ask myself if I've read, learned, or been exposed to this topic in the past." "Finally, if the topic is new, I could do a Google search or ask peers or adults what they know about it."
We do: The teacher provides a different prompt (such as a different story), and all students review the steps aloud.	All students respond orally: "We first need to look at the title and see if we know anything about the topic." "Then, we need to look at the cover, table of contents, and images and ask ourselves if we've heard about the topic before." "Finally, if the topic is new to us, we could ask the teacher, a friend, or look up the topic on the internet."
You do one: Students are provided with another text and then individually review and write down the steps with their responses.	All students write: "First, I am looking at the title, and I realize I don't know anything about this topic." "Then, I looked at the cover, table of contents, and images, and I still didn't know anything about this topic." "Finally, I realized I could look up this topic on the internet to learn a few essential things about the subject before I begin reading."
You do many: All students practice using the strategy with multiple texts.	All students write: Students apply the three steps to the different texts.

Shrink the Paragraph

Before beginning this strategy, or any strategy, it's best to ask students to give you their undivided attention. Typically, the teacher asks students to close their laptops, textbooks, or anything on their desk and put down their writing utensils. This may take a few minutes, but it's essential that students don't have distractions on their desks or in their hands. Table 2.7 presents this strategy and provides an example.

TABLE 2.7: Shrink the Paragraph Strategy

STEP IN THE PROCESS	EXPLANATION	EXAMPLE
I do	The teacher applies the strategy of talking aloud to model for the students, specifically articulating each of the steps.	Teacher: "The first thing I need to do is read the paragraph." (The teacher reads the paragraph aloud.) "The second thing I need to do is underline the action in the sentence." (The teacher underlines the action word / verb in the sentence.) "The third thing I need to do is circle the who or the what in the sentence." (The teacher circles the who or what in the sentence.) "The last thing I need to do is write down two essential facts about the who or the what in the sentence." (The teacher writes down two essential facts about the who or what in the sentence.)
We do	The teacher puts another similar example on the board, and all students simultaneously apply the strategy articulating each step.	Teacher: "What's the first step?" All students: "We need to read the paragraph." Teacher: "Good—let's read the paragraph out loud." Teacher: "What do we do next?" All students: "We need to underline the action word / verb in the sentence." Teacher: "Ok—let's do that together." All students: "The action word in the sentence is . . . ." Teacher: "What's the next step?" All students: "The next step is to circle the who or what of the sentence." Teacher: "Good. Let's find that together." All students: "The who or what of the sentence is . . ." Teacher: "What's the last step?" All students: "The last step is to list two essential facts about the who or what in the sentence."

continued →

STEP IN THE PROCESS	EXPLANATION	EXAMPLE
You do one	Each student gets an example similar to the examples the teacher has shown, and each student completes the strategy in writing on their own.	Students write out the steps while applying the strategy. Students would write: First step: I read the paragraph and underline the action words. Second step: Then, I circle the who or what of the sentence (who or what is doing the action). Third step: I highlight two important facts about the who or the what. Fourth step: Once I've done this for each sentence in the paragraph, I write a summary from all of the highlighted passages (the important facts about the who or the what).
You do many	At this point, the skill needs to become automatic so it can be offloaded, enabling the student to master higher level skills. To do this, a lot of correct practice is needed.	The teacher presents the students with many examples to practice the skill. Students would be presented with multiple paragraphs of a text, for example, and then follow the steps for each of the paragraphs.

Text Patterns

Another effective strategy for students to learn is the specific and unique text pattern of narrative and expository texts. The narrative text follows a sequence of setting, characters, initiating event, complication, further complication, resolution, and moral. The classroom teacher once again uses an explicit approach to teach this strategy.

1. The teacher names the strategy: "This strategy is called *identifying the narrative text structure.*"

2. The teacher teaches students the narrative text pattern.

3. **I do:** The teacher models the strategy by reading a short story aloud and identifying the different elements of the narrative. For example, the teacher might say, "I think this is a narrative because it tells a story. . . . Now, I am being introduced to the character." When getting to the setting, the teacher might say, "Oh, the story takes place in the forest." The teacher would continue reading and identify when the initiating event is presented by saying, "The family decided to go for a walk in the forest." The teacher explains that this is the initiating event because

it likely sets up the complication or conflict. The teacher continues to read, noting how the conflict increases in complexity until a climax is reached, at which point there is a resolution to the story.

4. **We do:** The teacher chooses another short story, reads it with students, and has all students in unison identify the text patterns by encouraging students to identify the text pattern simultaneously by calling out when each part is read.

5. **You do one:** The teacher gives each student a short story and has the students highlight each element of the narrative. Once completed, the teacher reviews the text pattern with the students. Students who are having difficulty would work with the teacher and receive a review of the steps. When a level of understanding is reached, they return to their seat and complete the process.

6. **You do many:** Students practice identifying the text features of narrative text with many different examples.

Teachers could provide students with cue cards of narrative text patterns such as *setting, characters, initiating event, complication or conflict, further complication or rising action, resolution,* and *moral.* The teacher can also provide signal words indicating the movement of the narrative from element to element. For example, terms such as *first, then, so,* and *finally* can be used.

Expository text has a different set of features. Expository texts characteristically follow one of the following text patterns.

1. **Cause and effect:** Events occur because of specific causes or causes are explained in terms of events, such as *Eli failed the exam because he didn't study.*

2. **Compare and contrast:** Text depicts how concepts, terms, ideas, or events are similar and different. Comparing periods, leaders, or cultures would fit into this text pattern.

3. **Description or attribution:** Text includes characteristics of a topic, idea, or event. For example, a description of an event or a natural disaster aligns with this text structure.

4. **Problem and solution:** A problem is presented with one or more solutions such as scientific or medical challenges and the solutions for these challenges. An example might be a text about a patient with high blood pressure who visited their doctor and received medication.

5. **Sequence:** Events are time-based or chronological. An example of this might be an explorer's three voyages to discover a new land, each voyage occurring at a specific date.

When teaching students expository text patterns, it's essential to teach them the words to look for in a text to identify the text pattern. For example, words like *because, since,* and *therefore* are commonly found in an expository text. Terms like *but, instead of,* and *however* are frequently found in a compare-and-contrast text. Descriptive text contains words like *such as* and *the characteristics are.* Problem and solution text has words like *since, so that,* and *a solution.* Finally, sequence text patterns have words like *first, second, then, after,* and *later.*

To teach text patterns of expository texts, begin by naming the strategy: "I will teach you a strategy to help you make sense of this expository fact-based text. You need to imagine that the author is sitting on your shoulder as you read. Throughout the reading of the text, you are asking the author questions about their intention when writing the text in the form of a text pattern."

Present students with one text type—for example, a descriptive text. Direct students to underline the key words commonly found in descriptive text. For example, they would underline words and phrases like *characteristics of, such as,* and *to illustrate,* which are commonly found in descriptive texts. Present students with one text pattern at a time and ask them to highlight the keywords associated with that text pattern. Additionally, present a visual organizer that students could use to reorganize the information from the text. Each text pattern has its own graphic organizer. Once the students have been explicitly taught the key features of each text pattern, present them with a multi-paragraph text where each paragraph would have a different text pattern. Here, students get key questions to help them identify the text pattern. For example, use questions such as *Is something being described?* and *Is there a problem presented and a solution?* Use the explicit teaching approach to teach students how to initially highlight the keywords in just one text pattern, such as descriptive, and then how to identify the text pattern when presented with multiple paragraphs and multiple text patterns. The explicit teaching approach should begin with *I do.* In the following example, the teacher uses a think-aloud during the I do step.

- **I do:** The teacher says, "When I read a fact-based text, I know that the author will teach me new information. I want to make sure that I know the specific message of that information presented in different text patterns. The first thing I need to do is read the text; I then need to read the text a second time, highlighting the keywords that will indicate the text pattern. If I see words like *characteristics of*, I will assume that the author is describing something. Then, I will draw the graphic organizer, write in the center what is being described, and, on the spokes, I will write down the characteristics using just a few words. If the concepts have primary and secondary features, I will draw smaller lines connected to those lines to indicate concepts and subconcepts."

The teacher draws and fills in the graphic organizer while explaining what they are doing.

- **We do:** The teacher, remaining with the same text pattern, shows another paragraph on the board, and this time, all students are expected to engage in this same task step by step. The teacher expects all students to recite the steps as the teacher writes the tasks on the board. Every student is expected to list the steps as they complete the task.

- **You do one:** The students each have a paragraph with a characteristic text pattern. The students follow the steps: they read the passage and then read it a second time, highlighting the words. They draw the graphic organizer for characteristic text patterns, writing the concept in the center and the descriptive characteristics on each spoke.

- **You do many:** Once the students can do one correctly, they work on doing this numerous times with different characteristic text patterns. The students who could not do one correctly work with the teacher. Once the students can do five paragraphs correctly, the teacher can assume they have mastered this skill with this one text pattern and then follow the same process with all five text patterns.

Reciprocal Teaching

Reciprocal teaching is another evidence-based strategy to support students' comprehension of text. Annemarie Sullivan Palincsar and Ann Brown (1984) sought to understand the methods good comprehenders use and teach those strategies to all students. Additionally, they strongly believed in the social nature of comprehension and the importance of students working collectively to make sense of the text. The reciprocal nature of comprehension is essential as students collaboratively comprehend text.

Palincsar and Brown (1984) identify that good comprehenders use the skills shown in table 2.8 when making sense of the text (Oczkus, 2018; Pilten, 2016).

TABLE 2.8: Skills Good Comprehenders Use to Understand Text

SKILL	DESCRIPTION
Predict	Use visual information such as the title, images, and charts to predict what the text is about.
Summarize	Summarize the text.
Question	Ask yourself questions to check for understanding.
Clarify	Clarify unclear information.
Predict	Predict what will come next based on the portion of the text read.

Follow the same explicit approach to guiding students to use reciprocal teaching as used in other strategies. Begin by naming the strategy. Explain that it's an effective approach to work collaboratively to make sense of expository text. Then, present the steps, ensuring that students process each step. You can do this by asking students to summarize each step in their own words. Next, follow the same explicit approach to teaching.

- **I do:** The teacher says, "The first thing we do when reading is to try to make sense of a text. We read the title, pictures, headings, and tables to predict what the text will be about." The teacher then talks aloud about the title and so on and predicts what she thinks the text will be about. She then says, "The second step is to read the first paragraph and then summarize the key elements of the text."

  The teacher explains that the summary should include only elements essential to the text. For example, if the text is about Sally, who fell down the stairs as she was rushing to get the school bus, the fact that she was wearing blue socks will likely not be essential to the text.

  The teacher then says, "The third thing we need to do is ask ourselves questions to check for our understanding." The teacher models asking questions, saying, for example, "Why did Sally fall?" The teacher then answers her question: "Because she was late for the bus."

  The teacher then says, "The fourth step is to clarify any unclear words or passages." The teacher models this by saying, "I don't know what *rushing* means; I should probably ask a friend or the teacher." At this point, the teacher wouldn't guide students to look up the word in a dictionary because this is a complex additional skill that would likely create cognitive overload when taught along with this new strategy of reciprocal teaching.

Finally, the teacher models predicting: "I think that the following paragraph is going to be about what happened to Sally after she fell."

- **We do:** Because there isn't one specific response to each of the steps in reciprocal teaching, the teacher would likely ask individual students to respond to each of the prompts (predict, summarize, question, clarify, and predict the upcoming paragraph) and provide detailed and guided feedback.

- **You do one:** The teacher then asks students to use these strategies on their own to ensure that they can follow this reciprocal teaching process.

- For the **you do many** stage, once students can complete the prompts with one paragraph, the teacher could put students in groups of four, ask each group member to take on the task of one of the reciprocal teaching steps, and have them engage in the dialogue.

For younger students in grades 1 or 2 who are not yet proficient readers, the teacher can read one passage aloud and engage students in the process, following each step in the reciprocal teaching process.

Adler's Close Reading

The final strategy is Adler's close reading strategy, which teaches students that reading comprehension is best when the text is read at least three times, each time with a different focus (Adler, 1940). The first reading is to get the general gist of the passage. The second reading is to identify the author's purpose. The goal of the third reading is to make connections between the text and the reader.

The teacher models the process using a step-by-step approach, explaining, "First, we need to read the passage and try to gain a global picture of what the text is about." Readers highlight difficult words and then draw a picture of the theme of the passage. The teacher then models reading the text a second time and asks questions such as *What was the author's purpose?* or *What is the text pattern?* The teacher then follows the process for a text pattern, reading the text a third time and asking questions enabling the reader to make connections. Figures 2.4, 2.5, and 2.6 (pages 58–59) are templates students use for the three readings of the text.

In the My Responses column, primary and early elementary students can draw pictures instead of responding in writing.

Prompts	My Responses
Overarching theme: I am predicting what I think the story will be about from the headings and pictures.	
After the first reading: Three key ideas are . . .	
I find these words difficult.	
Here's a picture of what I think the story is about.	

FIGURE 2.4: Adler's close reading template for first reading of the text.

Visit **go.SolutionTree.com/literacy** *to download the free reproducible version of this figure.*

Prompts	My Responses
List the interesting words and the words that repeat themselves.	
What am I thinking about as I read the story?	
Who is telling the story (an expert, a narrator, someone else)?	

FIGURE 2.5: Adler's close reading template for second reading of the text.

Prompts	My Responses
List the elements of the text. Narrative text Characters Setting Initiating event Problem Solution Moral	
Expository text:	

*Visit **go.SolutionTree.com/literacy** to download the free reproducible version of this figure.*

Prompts	My Responses
Why did the author write this story?	
This text reminds me of . . .	
Another story I read like this one was . . .	
This story reminds me of the time when I . . .	

FIGURE 2.6: Adler's close reading template for third reading of the text.

*Visit **go.SolutionTree.com/literacy** to download the free reproducible version of this figure.*

Conclusion

This chapter described each of the big 5 literacy elements, highlighted the importance of incorporating them into all classrooms, and provided specific strategies that should be implemented to ensure students are developing the essential elements of literacy. The next chapter focuses on reading and response to intervention—the early detection of reading challenges and effective intervention—which are critical factors to students' future success.

The Big 5 of Literacy: Next Steps

The Big 5	Strategies I'd like to try	Reflections
Phonemic Awareness		
Phonics		
Vocabulary		
Fluency		
Comprehension		

CHAPTER 3

READING AND RESPONSE TO INTERVENTION

Reading is the gateway to student success in school; if students struggle to read, they'll have difficulty accessing essential information required in all subjects—the information required for success in school. According to Austin Buffum, Mike Mattos, and Janet Malone (2018) in *Taking Action: A Handbook for RTI at Work*, "Success in school is the factor that most directly predicts the length and quality of students' lives" (p. 1). They go on to say that "a student who fails to succeed in our K–12 system is three times more likely to be unemployed, sixty-three times more likely to be incarcerated and, on average, lives at least a decade shorter than a college graduate" (Buffum et al., 2018, p. 1). Furthermore, the joy readers experience in reading—from learning new and fascinating information or going on a fanciful journey in the pages of a book—will, sadly, evade them.

Early detection of reading challenges and effective intervention are critical factors to students' future success in school and beyond. Students who struggle to read in the early grades are far less likely to become proficient readers. Three quarters of students who are not reading in early elementary school remain poor readers throughout high school, not because they are inherently unable to read, but because formal reading instruction typically ends by this time. Thus, they do not have the opportunity to become proficient decoders before they are expected to reach higher-level comprehension (Annie E. Casey Foundation, 2010).

During the early years of school, students *learn to read*, but once they begin the middle grades, they *read to learn*, meaning they must now use their reading skills to glean information from all sorts of texts. Mastering reading goes far beyond reading in language classes; it requires reading texts in all disciplines, such as mathematics, history, and geography. Students must be able to parse written text—decode it and read with fluency and ease to discern meaning. Therefore, effective instruction at all grade levels is paramount; students from kindergarten to the end of grade 3 need to master decoding, fluency, and basic comprehension, and in the higher grades, starting in middle school, students need to become proficient comprehenders. Response to Intervention (RTI) is a highly valuable model to ensure effective instruction for all and identify students at risk of not achieving proficiency. This chapter begins with information on the challenging history for intervention practices before outlining strategies for reading support and intervention in the three tiers of the RTI model.

A Challenging History for Intervention Practices

Before the reauthorization of the Individuals with Disabilities Education Improvement Act (IDEIA) in 2004, students had to show a significant discrepancy between their performance and IQ to qualify for special education services (Restori, Katz, & Lee, 2009). This notion was problematic for many reasons. First, the assumption was that only students with at least an average IQ should be considered to have a learning disability and benefit from intervention to close their learning gap. According to Elliott and Grigorenko (2014), this faulty notion originated from the belief that "IQ tests provide a picture of fixed potential that places a limit on academic potential" (p. 19). Sir Cyril Burt (1937) blatantly articulated this belief by saying that "capacity must obviously limit content. It is impossible for a pint jug to hold more than a pint of milk, and it is equally impossible for a child's educational attainment to rise higher than his educable capacity" (Burt, 1937, p. 477; Elliott & Grigorenko, 2014). A second, equally problematic byproduct of the discrepancy model was that students needed to show a significant gap between their performance and grade-level expectations before receiving intervention services. According to longitudinal research conducted by Sally Shaywitz and Bennett Shaywitz (2005) and Shaywitz, Morris, & Shaywitz (2008), only a percentage of students with low reading scores meet the discrepancy model; thus, the remaining weak readers do not have scores that are weak enough to enable them entry into resource support programs. This was called the "wait to fail" model because students had to wait to reach a level of significant failure before being eligible to receive intervention services (Shaywitz et al., 2008; Shaywitz & Shaywitz, 2005).

In response to the problematic wait-to-fail model in IDEA, there was a reauthorization of the Individuals with Disabilities Education Improvement Act (IDEIA) that abandoned the criterion for identification and intervention for students with reading challenges (Johnston, 2011). The new service delivery model, response to intervention, marked a significant shift in how and when schools could identify and support students with challenges. This model reinforces the need for early assessment based on easy-to-implement curriculum-based measures and evidence-based instruction (Dougherty Stahl, 2016).

Response to Intervention

RTI is a multitiered model of effective teaching and early intervention for all students. Because this book focuses on reading, I address RTI with a focus on literacy. RTI is made up of three tiers, as shown in figure 3.1. Tier 1 is effective core classroom instruction for all students. Tier 2 is a support structure for students who are not progressing sufficiently to close the gap between their current level and the grade-level benchmark and thus need additional reading intervention. Tier 3 is for students who are significantly below grade level and require intensive support (Barrio, Lindo, Combes, & Hovey, 2015).

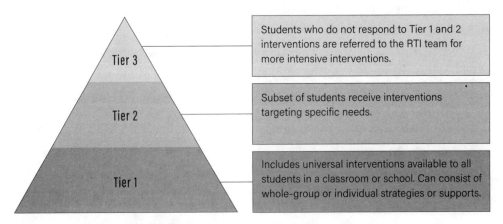

Source: Adapted from Buffum, Mattos, & Weber, 2012, p. 13.

FIGURE 3.1: RTI pyramid of interventions.

Tier 1

Tier 1 of the RTI pyramid includes (1) evidence-based teaching, (2) universal screening, (3) in-class remedial supports for students at risk, and (4) progress monitoring.

Evidence-Based Teaching

Evidence-based teaching is teaching using materials and practices that have been researched to be effective at teaching students to read. Despite increasing knowledge about evidence-based teaching practices, teachers often persist in using materials from sources that are not founded in the research. With the advent of social media and the ease at which teachers can share sources with one another, it has become increasingly challenging to distinguish between evidence-based practice and materials not founded in evidence or research. It is insufficient, however, to depend only on the research; evidence is required that the reading methods and practices being implemented are effective within the classroom (Shaywitz & Shaywitz, 2005).

Universal Screening

All students, typically from kindergarten to the end of middle school (grade 8), are assessed using universal screening tools such as DIBELS, Aimsweb, Renaissance, or Acadience to ensure that they are attaining grade-level benchmarks. In addition, schools and teachers use curriculum-based tools for assessment because they address the curricular goals that students are expected to master at each grade level. Universal screening tools are easily available but can appear daunting to teachers at first. Because these tools are normed, teachers need to be consistent in the delivery and assessment of these tools to ensure fidelity of grading thus enabling teachers to make accurate decisions about students' needs based on these assessments. Regardless of which assessment tool teachers use, schools must assess all fundamental reading skills. These skills include the following:

- Phonemic awareness (blending, segmenting, and manipulating the individual sounds in a word)
- Phonics (decoding or associating the letter to its component sound)
- Vocabulary (knowledge of word meanings in isolation and in a text)
- Fluency (reading quickly, without error and with proper cadence)
- Reading comprehension (understanding text read by the reader)

As students progress through the grades, the target goals and benchmarks increase accordingly. In the early grades, students are assessed on phonemic awareness, letter naming, and decoding, but higher-level skills such as fluency and comprehension become the focus as students move into middle school (typically grades 3 and higher).

With the universal screening tools, teachers themselves can assess their students' reading skills, and they don't need to wait for costly psycho-educational assessments.

Teachers need to be empowered with the ability to assess their own students using these curriculum-based measures and provide in-class support to those not mastering grade-level reading skills. For far too long, teachers have been led to believe that the assessment of essential skills for students at risk required a specialization they didn't possess. This belief is both faulty and damaging to the success of students. There are typically long waiting lists for formal assessments. Additionally, they are usually costly and lead to an undervaluing of the capacity of the classroom teacher.

In-Class Remedial Supports for Students Below Reading Benchmark

The third component of Tier 1 is that students with reading achievement moderately below the benchmark or significantly below the benchmark should receive in-class remediation. Providing remedial intervention in the classroom is a challenge that teachers cannot overlook. It is important for teachers to find time in their daily schedules to provide individual students or the whole class with targeted intervention based on universal screening results. Teachers also need to become knowledgeable about different evidence-based reading strategies.

The most effective way to offer in-class support is to group students based on their reading strengths and weaknesses—in other words, differentiating their instruction—at least for a targeted period each day. (Many of these strategies are presented in this book.) Even twenty minutes of support daily would enable the classroom teacher to reinforce much-needed targeted skill development. Students at level based on the universal screening results work independently on grade-level material, such as comprehension work (reading and responding to questions) or writing responses (based on a text). Students assessed as below grade level on a specific skill would be grouped according to the target skill and receive additional support in the areas of weakness (letter naming, phonemic awareness, phonics, fluency, vocabulary, or comprehension). The strategies for the big 5 of literacy identified in the previous chapter can be applied more intensely to these students.

Progress Monitoring

Progress monitoring is the ongoing assessment tool used to ascertain if the focused support is effective at closing the gap resulting in students' mastery of the identified weak skills. (Progress monitoring occurs in all three tiers.) It could appear daunting for teachers unfamiliar with these types of ongoing, norm-based assessments where specific instructions must be adhered to and assessments must be conducted according to the form laid out in the manual. Also, the challenge could arise with finding time within the Tier 1 classroom to conduct progress monitoring. However, with limited practice, teachers can become experts in the domain of progress monitoring. And more important, decisions about what types of support are required to close learning gaps will become clear to the teacher.

The curriculum-based assessments mentioned in the previous section also include progress monitoring probes—like universal screening but with multiple prompts or examples to assess skills more often. For instance, if phonemic awareness is the target skill, the probes would include words that need to be segmented into sounds. If fluency is the skill being remediated, progress monitoring assessments would provide numerous examples of student-proficiency with short fluency passages.

For the sake of clarity, let's look at a specific example. Figure 3.2 shows the fluency scores of a class of grade 6 students. At the start of the grade 6 year, students' fluency scores should fall within the range of 123–150 correct words per minute. In the example, only three students' scores fell within this range. Therefore, the teachers would engage in a repeated reading strategy to increase the oral reading fluency rate of these grade 6 students.

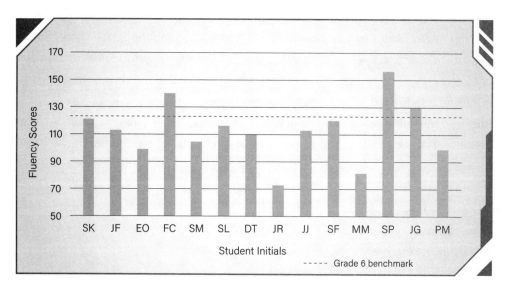

FIGURE 3.2: Oral reading fluency scores of grade 6 Tier 1 students in September.

However, as you can see in figure 3.3, after Tier 1, in-class interventions, the majority of students fall within the benchmark.

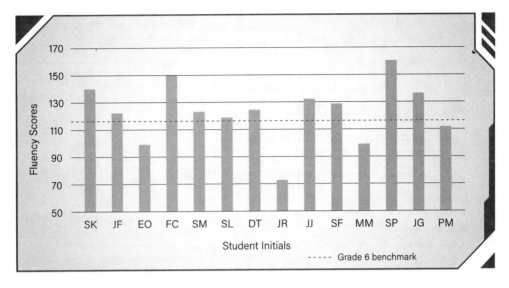

FIGURE 3.3: Oral Reading scores of Tier 1 students after a few months of intervention.

Tier 2

The information gleaned from the progress monitoring assessment provides essential information on the student's progress. Of important note here is that mere progress is not sufficient. A student, Rachel, may show improvement but remain significantly below the grade-level benchmark. In general, the student's progress must indicate that the gap between their reading scores and the grade-level benchmark is decreasing. Figure 3.4 (page 70) shows that whereas Rachel is improving, her improvement is not sufficient to close the gap.

In figure 3.4 (page 70), Rachel was not showing sufficient progress in Tier 1 as compared to the benchmark line. However, when provided with additional Tier 2 support, the improvement level shows that the gap is closing (see figure 3.5, page 70).

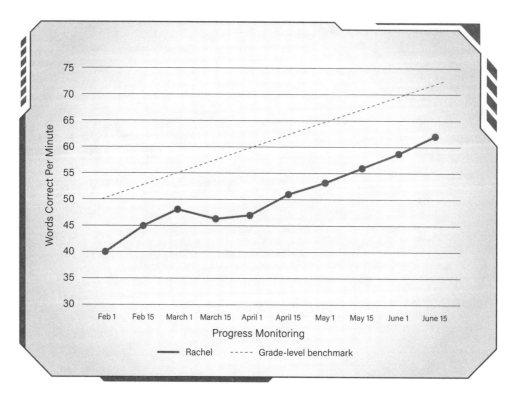

FIGURE 3.4: Tier 1 progress monitoring showing insufficient progress indicating student requires additional Tier 2 support.

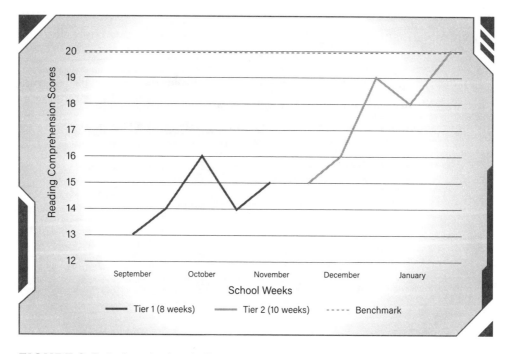

FIGURE 3.5: Student showing significant progress in Tier 2.

Students who do not show sufficient improvement and thus continue to be at risk with reading development need more learning time with a qualified educator. These students should receive Tier 2 additional intervention in reading during *non-core instruction* for around thirty to forty-five minutes three times per week. This point is critical and often results in a misunderstanding in the application of RTI. In some schools and school districts, students who are weak in reading receive remediation during their core reading instruction period.

To exemplify why this is problematic, suppose you have two students in your class—student A and student B. Student A is reading well below the benchmark and struggling to decode basic text. In contrast, student B is a strong reader, mastering all grade-level expectations. Student A receives sixty minutes of remedial support outside the class during the sixty-minute core instruction period. During that time, student B is in the class receiving sixty minutes of core instruction with the classroom teacher. In that case, students A and B would receive the same amount of reading time despite their different needs. To close a reading gap, the student who is struggling needs more instructional time than students at benchmark, and with a qualified reading teacher. Therefore, struggling students need to remain in Tier 1 classroom instruction in addition to receiving additional help. Schools can be creative about the time of day chosen for this remediation. For example, schools can provide the support during an instated period 0, offer a supplementary period before the official school day begins, or reduce each period by five minutes. This enables them to add a thirty-minute block (if there are six periods in the day) that can be used for completing homework, locker cleaning, or additional reading support.

Furthermore, Tier 2 remedial intervention must be evidence-based and provided in small groups—as long as all students receive support in the area of weakness as indicated in the universal screening and progress monitoring assessments. Progress monitoring must be conducted in Tier 2 as well. Students who show progress on the identified skill will continue in Tier 2 until they have mastered the target skill. Once they have mastered the skill, they move out of Tier 2, and their space is available for other students requiring additional reading support.

Tier 3

Tier 2 students who are not showing mastery of the target skill after approximately eight weeks need more intensive Tier 3 support. The primary difference between Tier 2 and Tier 3 is the intensity of the support and the grouping. Tier 3 support is typically provided one-on-one and daily for forty-five minutes to an hour (or as often as possible within the constraints of the schedule and support available). However, the intervention method and materials don't necessarily need to be different than those provided in Tier 2. Progress monitoring is required to ensure that the intervention approach is successful and students are showing sufficient progress. To close the gap, students must demonstrate a gradual but consistent increase in reading, leading them toward grade-level expectations.

The RTI model looks somewhat different beyond the upper elementary level. RTI implementation in middle and high school is more challenging, primarily because students have many teachers, making it more difficult to collaborate around students' needs (Epler, 2017).

One significant difference is the luxury of time at the elementary level, which is often not prevalent in high school. For example, when students are assessed as at risk in elementary school, they can receive remedial support in Tier 1 while the teacher keeps a watchful eye on them. Eight weeks is an appropriate time to wait before deciding if an elementary student needs supplementary intervention. However, students whose needs weren't addressed in the early grades will likely be more at risk. Consequently, high school students should receive Tier 2 or Tier 3 support early in the year, perhaps immediately following the universal screening results. Again, schools need to be creative in finding additional time for remedial support so students can remain in their core instruction class while also receiving supplemental targeted support.

Examination of Instructional Practice

RTI is a highly effective model to support all students and provide just-on-time intervention to those struggling to master foundational skills. The model is not in any way aimed at blaming teachers or making teachers feel inadequate for not ensuring all students have acquired grade-level skills proficiency. It is, however, meant to encourage teachers to examine their instructional practices to ensure they lead to academic success for most students and that students who are not achieving success are identified and supported (Benedict, Brownell, Bettini, & Sohn, 2021; Epler, 2017).

Researcher John Hattie examined 1,400 meta-analyses of almost 83,000 studies identifying 250 factors impacting students' success, including RTI (Hattie & Zierer, 2019). The concept of effect size was used to highlight the effectiveness of each of the strategies. This measure is often used to indicate the amount of student growth attributed to a particular strategy; the higher the effect size, the stronger the relationship between the two variables or two conditions. Effect size is often used to assess the effectiveness of an intervention because it provides information about whether an intervention is effective in increasing student outcomes and to what extent or how much growth can be expected. Jacob Cohen (1988) created a formula to quantify the strength of an intervention: Cohen's *d*. According to Cohen (1988), 0.2 is a small effect size, 0.5 is a medium effect size, and 0.8 is a substantial effect size. For example, a 0.2 effect size would indicate a minimal difference of one group of students compared to a control group that didn't receive the specific intervention. Of Hattie's 250 factors, some are highly positive and others highly negative. For example, the most effective factor with an effect size of 1.57 is collective teacher efficacy, which supports the importance of school-based professional development. Interestingly, the most negative factor leading to poor student outcomes is students with ADHD, with an effect size of −0.90, presumably for students who were not adequately supported (Hattie & Zierer, 2019).

Three meta-analyses were included in Hattie's RTI examination, totaling fifty-eight research studies. RTI is among the top five most influential factors, leading to positive student outcomes with an effect size of 1.34, indicating that the average student in a school that incorporates an RTI model scores 1.34 standard deviations higher than the average student in the control group (students not implicated by RTI; Hattie, 2012). Longitudinal studies further show that a typical effect size for classroom instruction ranges from 0.15 to 0.40 (Buffum et al., 2018). Thus, 1.34 indicates significant student growth. It's important to note that effect size does not imply causality but rather a relationship between two factors (the experimental and control group).

Essential Principles for RTI Practices

RTI was promulgated as a response to a damaging wait-to-fail model that required many students to wait years before receiving reading remediation because their reading scores on assessment measures were not weak enough. Despite the many research studies positing the effectiveness of RTI, it remains controversial and often misunderstood. According to Katherine Dougherty Stahl (2016), in her article "Response to Intervention: Is the Sky Falling?," discrepancies in student outcomes were found in samples that followed a research-based approach and adhered to the principles of RTI compared to schools that had not.

According to a large-scale study conducted by Rekha Balu, Pei Zhu, Fred Dolittle, Ellen Schiller, Joseph Jenkins, and Russell Gersten (2015), there were marked differences in adherence to RTI guidelines when schools implemented RTI on their own compared to schools that were part of a research study. Schools that independently implemented RTI interpreted its practices without including essential elements of the model, such as full core instruction time for all students, especially those at risk for academic challenges. Moreover, the National Center for Education Evaluation and Regional Assistance examined the progress of thousands of early elementary students' reading scores, and the results indicated that students who received RTI tiered interventions did worse on their reading scores than those who didn't receive support (as cited by Buffum et al., 2018). However, according to Buffum and colleagues, when RTI is used to identify students for special education services immediately without empowering the classroom teacher to support these students in the regular classroom, or when it's used to address the past failure of over-identifying minority groups in special education, it will not reach its full potential.

Whether implemented under the guidance of research expertise or independently, there are seven essential principles that schools must include in all RTI practices.

1. Universal screening

2. Data-based, collaborative decision making

3. Evidence-based classroom instruction

4. Differentiation

5. Progress monitoring

6. Multitiered supports

7. Evidence-based remedial supports for students at minimal or significant risk

Universal Screening

Universal screening must be conducted at least twice a year and optimally three times a year. These screenings are not the ultimate word of who does and doesn't receive additional support, but they contribute to an overall picture of student performance and mastery of grade-level outcomes.

Data-Based, Collaborative Decision Making

Data-based collaborative decision making is essential as it provides a basis on which decisions are made about student performance. Based on years of research, there is broad consensus that the big 5 of literacy (phonemic awareness, phonics, vocabulary, fluency, and comprehension) are essential components of reading proficiency. Therefore, data should be used to ascertain if students are reaching grade-level expectations of these elements. If not, schools should use the data to craft remedial support for the target students. These decisions shouldn't be based on one teacher's examination of the data but should include input from multiple teachers.

Evidence-Based Classroom Instruction

Evidence-based instruction highlights the importance of ensuring that Tier 1 materials and instructional practices are founded in research and shown to be effective in the classroom. Effective classroom instruction must be the primary focus. I strongly suggest that schools committed to implementing RTI invest in strengthening classroom instruction. Providing remedial support to students when core instruction is lacking can be likened to building a second or third level to your house when the foundation is weak.

Far too often, classroom instruction is absent of evidence-based materials and methods, leaving teachers dependent on materials that are neither evidence-based (incorporating the big 5) nor adherent to a scope and sequence of instruction that effectively teaches the big 5 of literacy. John Hattie's (Hattie & Zierer, 2019) research on the most effective practices will undoubtedly benefit student outcomes. As explained in the previous section, Hattie (Hattie & Zierer, 2019) identified a set of instructional factors that have a powerful impact on student learning. In addition to collective teacher efficacy, these factors include clarity of goals, teacher clarity, student feedback, metacognitive strategies, and mnemonics, to name just a few. RTI must be based on a solid teaching foundation in the Tier 1 classroom (Hattie & Zierer, 2019). Robert Marzano also identifies effective strategies teachers should use to enhance student learning. These strategies include providing and communicating learning goals, using multiple forms of assessment, direct instruction, and teaching cross-curricular strategies that transfer from one discipline to another, such as note-taking and communicating high expectations (Marzano, 2017).

Differentiation

Differentiated practice is the fourth essential principle that should be part of all RTI implementation. Differentiation is both a concept and a practice. As a concept, differentiation is a value that highlights the belief that all students deserve to have their academic, behavioral, and social needs met in the classroom (Gazith, 2021). With this belief comes the need to operationalize differentiation. For example, when a teacher meets with a small group of students struggling with a specific comprehension strategy while other students practice the strategy, the teacher engages in differentiation.

Progress Monitoring

The fifth principle is ongoing progress monitoring. Targeted support, whether provided in Tier 1, 2, or 3, is only useful if it leads to student growth—and the only way to assess growth is through progress monitoring. Progress monitoring refers to regular check-ins with students, approximately once every few weeks, to ascertain if the intervention is closing the learning gap. For example, if we go back to our fluency example, suppose in February, a grade 3 student, John, is reading 40 words per minute correctly. The benchmark score for a grade 3 student mid-year is between the range of 50–64; thus, a score of 40 would indicate that this student is at risk for fluency, which impacts his reading comprehension and likely will continue to do so (Price, Meisinger, Louwerse, & D'Mello, 2016).

Therefore, this student would need an intervention, such as the repeated reading strategy (see page 46) to improve his reading fluency. However, progress monitoring is required to assess if his fluency is improving. Every two weeks or so, the student's progress should be monitored by assessing his words per minute on a grade 2-level text (to align the text more closely with his reading level), to assess if his reading rate has increased. Yet only looking at an increase in score is insufficient because while he is improving, the number of words expected per minute for a grade 3 student also increases. Even though the student is practicing his fluency using a grade 2-level text and progress monitoring is being conducted on a grade 2-level text, you want to examine if the gap between the student's current reading level and grade-level expectation is decreasing. Therefore, as you examine the progress monitoring scores of a student with reading challenges, it's essential to examine the trend line to ensure that the gap between the grade-level expectation and the student score is decreasing. No specific score is required; it is simply to examine the data and judge based on the trend line as to whether the student is making sufficient progress.

Multitiered Supports

The sixth essential principle is a multitiered support structure. All schools must be organized such that students' level of support is commensurate with their needs. Students progressing according to grade-level expectations continue to receive academic instruction in the classroom only. Students who are showing signs of risk and not reaching the benchmark for their grade level receive additional support in Tier 1 that supplements but doesn't supplant core reading instruction. Intensive support is reserved for students showing significant risk and who are substantially below where they should be for their grade level despite effective classroom reading instruction. Worth noting here is that an effective RTI support delivery model must include Tier 3 intensive support for the 5 percent of students at serious risk with reading. Tier 3 remedial support is more challenging because it is more costly and time-consuming. However, despite the additional complexity of Tier 3 support, it can't and shouldn't be overlooked. Reading problems don't disappear and, with time, only worsen. As the adage goes, *you pay now or later*; a significant investment will need to be made. If not addressed early on, the investment required will increase both in terms of time and financial resources, not to mention the cost to the student whose struggle will be commensurate with the increased expectations at higher grade levels.

Evidence-Based Remedial Supports

The final essential principle of RTI is that all remedial supports must be evidence-based and provided by a reading specialist or at least overseen by someone with expertise in supporting struggling readers. All students will show some sign of progress merely from working with an adult, but sheer progress is insufficient. There is a renaissance in educational research that can guide teachers in identifying effective remedial support. There are many effective, evidence-based remedial programs for struggling readers in all tiers (Epler, 2017), such as Peer-Assisted Learning Strategies (PALS), Read 180, Accelerated Reader, Fast ForWord, SpellRead, Cooperative Integrated Reading and Composition, Reciprocal Teaching, ReadingPlus, Repeated Reading. McGraw Hill has an excellent list of these and other remedial reading programs (mheducation.com).

Conclusion

RTI is a solid, logical, and evidence-based school support model that incorporates practices that have long been identified as critical to the success of all students.

Students deserve to learn in a classroom that prioritizes reading instruction and mastery and provides early and effective support to students who are struggling.

The next chapter examines how schools and teachers should intervene and provide support for students with reading challenges.

Reading and Response to Intervention: Next Steps

The RTI Principle	What I can do to implement this principle?	Reflections
Universal screening		
Data-based, collaborative decision making		
Evidence-based classroom instruction		
Differentiation		
Progress monitoring		
Multitiered supports		
Evidence-based remedial supports for students at minimal or significant risk		

CHAPTER 4

MODELS FOR READING SUPPORT

Every new school year typically starts with universal screening of students. Teachers are often perplexed and concerned with screening results that indicate a high number of students who haven't yet mastered their grade-level expectations. In reading, some students have mastered decoding, but their poor fluency or comprehension skills put them mildly or significantly at risk. In addition, they might have difficulty because of limited vocabulary development; they don't understand vocabulary that is essential to understanding grade-level texts (such as novels) or content-area texts (such as science books). Unfortunately, despite the number of students who struggle to read, reading instruction often fades away after grade three (Wanzek, Vaughn, Scammacca, Metz, Murray, Roberts, & Danielson, 2013). Furthermore, low-income students often experience a slump in their reading in grade 4 despite initially being at grade level for reading, which puts them at additional risk (Wanzek et al., 2013).

Providing reading support to students at any age can be a significant challenge for schools, but students must receive this support, regardless of a student's grade level. This chapter highlights models for providing support for students who are not reaching grade-level literacy benchmarks.

Responding to Diversity in Reading Levels

According to the National Assessment of Educational Progress (NAEP), "Reading is an active and complex process that involves: (a) understanding text, (b) developing and interpreting meaning, and (c) using meaning as appropriate to type of text, purpose, and situation" (NAEP, 2013). The NAEP (2022) finds that only 36 percent of fourth-grade students and 26 percent of eighth-grade students are at or above proficiency in reading. Reading scores declined in more than half the states in the

United States, and only one in four students demonstrated proficiency in reading (NAEP, 2022). Reading scores were lower than all prior assessment years since 2005 for fourth graders and lower than all scores since 1998 for eighth graders. In eighth grade, the average reading score was lower than all previous assessment years going back to 1998. The decline in reading scores compared to 2019 was consistent for almost all states in the United States.

In light of the increasing number of students struggling with reading, teachers need to not only teach their curriculum but also provide intervention to students who are significantly below grade level. Maintaining this balance between teaching the curriculum and providing remedial reading support to students with significant reading gaps can be extremely challenging. Additionally, finding the time to do this and identifying the structures that allow for a high level of differentiation between students places great pressure on teachers. As Alex Quigley (2020) articulates, "Despite reading proving the master skill of school, teachers receive too little high-quality training on teaching reading" (p. 10).

To better understand how classrooms can respond to the increasing diversity in students' reading levels, let's dispel some myths about poor performance. The first myth is that most readers with poor reading skills struggle to read due to poor comprehension. In reality, most of these struggling readers, especially those in higher grades, exhibit poor comprehension primarily because of their insufficient mastery of basic reading skills, such as accurate and rapid reading (Nation, 2019). Another common belief is that readers struggle because they lack motivation or need to work harder. Poor readers often work extremely hard to keep up with grade-level expectations. When students with reading challenges appear to give up, they may be doing so because they have not experienced the benefits of their hard work—sometimes for years (Toste, Didion, Peng, Filderman, & McClelland, 2020).

The third and perhaps most concerning myth is that teachers can identify nonreaders without screening tools. Students with dyslexia often have strong visual memories, so educators may mistakenly believe that they are reading (decoding) when, in fact, they are visually memorizing the word. This is why all students should be screened using curriculum-based measures such as DIBELS (Butler, 2022).

Accommodations Versus Remediation

Schools and educators hope that foundational reading instruction in the early grades will suffice to ensure that all students become proficient readers. Unfortunately, this is often not a reality, and once students reach grade 3, reading instruction generally ends, and students are expected to have mastered basic reading skills that enable them to comprehend more complex texts. Many students, approximately 20 percent, will struggle to learn to read (Moats, 2020). According to a report of the Institute of Education Sciences: National Center for Special Education Research, "Children who do not read well are more likely to be retained a grade in school, drop out of high school, become teen parents, or enter the juvenile justice system" (Connor, Alberto, Compton, & O'Connor, 2014, p. 1). Therefore, regardless of age or severity of challenge, all students should receive reading support within or outside the classroom.

In my work with schools and at literacy conferences, I inevitably receive questions about accommodations and remediation, and when and how to implement each. The question of whether accommodations and remediation are synonymous is also common.

It is important to differentiate between *accommodations* and *remediation*, as they are not the same thing. Accommodations provide adjustments to the learning or evaluation environment to help students succeed in meeting the criteria; remediation involves providing reading interventions for struggling students. Both remediation and accommodation are needed to level the playing field for students with reading challenges.

Models of Support for Students

The range of student reading proficiency varies greatly within any given classroom, from first grade until the end of high school (Missall, Hosp, & Hosp, 2019). Because student proficiency levels vary, the first step in supporting readers who are below proficiency is to identify them by assessing student reading levels. Maddie Witter (2013) uses an exercise analogy to explain the need for such identification when she states, "Trying to bench press 150 pounds doesn't make me stronger" (p. 25); reading can only improve if students read at or close to their proficiency level (Hoover & Tunmer, 2018). Just as someone who is beginning weight-lifting training will get no benefit from attempting to lift weights that are way too heavy, students lacking reading skills won't get any benefit out of attempting to read text way above their proficiency level. Therefore, identifying student proficiency levels is an essential first step to providing intervention and support to struggling students.

The best way to determine student proficiency levels is to begin with the corresponding grade-level assessment on the universal screening tool, such as DIBELS, Acadience, Renaissance, and Aimsweb. Students who are either at risk or significantly below grade level should then be evaluated on a lower grade assessment—a process called *testing down*. This process continues until the student is reading at the level based on the screening tool. For example, a student in grade 6 may be significantly at risk on the grade 6 universal screening assessment. The assessor, who is usually the classroom teacher, then assesses the student on lower grade-level assessments. For example, the student would be assessed on a grade 5 assessment, and if they were still below the benchmark, a grade 4 assessment is conducted. Testing down continues until the student's results show them at the level for that grade. This is the vital information a teacher needs regarding the student's current reading level and the skills they need to progress to grade-level proficiency.

Having the correct information is critical for teachers to support students' reading development in the classroom. To help readers at risk, teachers implement intervention practices that allow for differentiation. For students below grade level, this intervention is not meant to supplant additional Tier 2 or Tier 3 support (see chapter 3, page 63) but rather to supplement it. The following sections present a variety of models suited to providing support to students with learning gaps in reading: acceleration, anchor activities, push-in and pull-out, and accommodations are the practices covered in the following sections.

Acceleration

The acceleration model involves a series of steps to provide students with reading challenges with the fundamental skills they need a few days before they are taught in the classroom (Pepper Rollins, 2014). What students already know when they enter the classroom impacts their learning significantly, and past gaps impact current learning. We must ensure, therefore, that small gaps do not grow into large ones that are hard to close. This concern is best articulated by Marzano (2004), who states, "What students already know when they enter the classroom—before we even meet them—is the strongest predictor of how well they will learn the new curriculum" (as cited in Pepper Rollins, 2014, p. 4). Acceleration focuses on preventing student failure in the first place; this model could help at least some students avoid years of accumulated gaps.

With the acceleration model, students with learning gaps receive preteaching of strategies so that when core Tier 1 learning takes place, they have the much-needed advantage of being familiar with the content. This additional support occurs either before the school day, during lunch, after school, during a period 0 or any time the school could find within or outside of the schedule to provide support, or, in rare cases, during the weekend.

Approximately twice a week, students receive forty-five minutes of support so they can be a class or two ahead of their classmates. This model is intended for students who are slightly below the benchmark and is best applied with what is referred to as *bubble students,* or students not yet displaying significant challenges (Mulcahey, 2018). The goal is to give them an advantage before they begin to experience more significant gaps.

This model includes six steps.

1. Present a hook or entry point.

2. Establish learning goals and communicate them to the student.

3. Fill essential gaps.

4. Teach key vocabulary.

5. Teach the new concept or skill.

6. Formatively assess student.

Present a Hook

The first step is to present the student with a hook or an entry point related to the topic. For example, teachers are working on a particular reading comprehension strategy, such as reciprocal teaching. The teacher asks the student what the story is about based on the title page of a book or headings in a chapter. The teacher then explains to the student that he or she will learn about a strategy that incorporates prediction and that this strategy is beneficial in helping the student understand the reading. This sets the stage for what the student will learn and provides context or purpose for the learning. This strategy would be appropriate for students of all ages, but the language used to guide students would need to be matched to their age and grade level.

Establish and Communicate Learning Goals

The second step in the acceleration process is to establish learning goals and communicate these goals to the student. Communicate to students what specific knowledge they'll need to know by the end of the lesson and what they'll be able to do with that knowledge, or what skill or subskill they will master. Continuing our example of reciprocal teaching, the teacher might say, "By the end of our acceleration lesson, you will know the steps of reciprocal teaching, and you'll be able to read a short passage and apply these steps."

Fill Essential Gaps

The third stage is to take a step back and fill in essential gaps. For example, if there are specific terms that the student is expected to know, such as *prediction* or *clarification*, they are taught at this step. Additionally, the teacher may provide the student with a scaffolding device, such as a handout featuring the reciprocal teaching steps.

Teach Key Vocabulary

The fourth step is teaching the student essential vocabulary words necessary to engage in the new strategy. In this case, the teacher may have chosen a specific text the student will use to practice reciprocal teaching. By introducing the essential vocabulary words in the text, the teacher prepares the student to apply reciprocal teaching.

Teach the New Concept or Skill

The fifth step involves teaching the new concept or skill. Here, the teacher introduces the reciprocal teaching steps to students, reviews them, models them, and engages in a reciprocal teaching dialogue. The student will already have these steps written out. Once the process has been modeled, the teacher and student practice reciprocal teaching using several paragraphs from an appropriate level text.

Formatively Assess Student

The final step in the process is formative assessment. The student applies reciprocal teaching to a short passage. A benefit of accelerated learning is that when the strategy is introduced in class to all students, this student will already be familiar with it.

Anchor Activities

Using anchor activities is another way to support learners who are struggling. After completing classwork, students who are proficient work independently on an anchor activity while teachers support struggling students. Imagine that the teacher has just taught specific graphemes in a phonics lesson or highlighted essential words in a vocabulary lesson. The teacher might introduce new strategies during the presentation and have students practice them through in-class activities. Students would likely fall into three groups: (1) Those who complete the activity quickly and are ready to move on, (2) students who need more time to complete the activity, and (3) students who need additional guidance from the classroom teacher. Students who complete the activity get an anchor activity and will be occupied, enabling students who need more time to complete the task under less pressure. Those who require remedial support from the classroom teacher will receive it in a smaller group. Once the concept or strategy is clear, they can return to their seat and complete their work.

In early elementary school, for example, if the students are learning letter sounds, a good anchor activity might be to create a book of words associated with the sounds learned. For middle elementary, the class activity may be to read a paragraph and identify the main ideas using a specific strategy such as Peer-Assisted Learning Strategy (PALS). The anchor activity might be to write out the steps to PALS with images that classmates can use. In middle school, a lesson on figurative language might consist of anchor activities that ask students to create a manual with illustrations explaining each type of figurative language with examples. Another anchor activity could be to create test questions for an upcoming test on figurative language. In high school, after a science lab, students may participate in an anchor activity in which they create a research study proposal based on the information they learned and the observations they made during the science lab.

Push-in and Pull-out

The next model to consider is push-in and pull-out supports to ensure that students below grade level receive the timely assistance needed. Typically, schools think of remedial help for students as either support provided by the classroom teacher within the class context or remedial support delivered by a remedial teacher outside of the class. However, classrooms can incorporate both push-in support in the classroom and pull-out support outside of the classroom (Demo, Nes, Somby, Frizzarin, & Dal Sovo, 2021). Specifically, the push-in model refers to the remedial teacher (an educator with experience teaching reading) who works with individual or small groups of students in the classroom. The classroom teacher and the remedial teacher can collaborate effectively to support students. Practically speaking, the classroom teacher determines certain times during the week for independent work so that both teachers can work productively without the remedial teacher having to talk over the teacher's voice. During this period, the classroom teacher guides the remedial teacher about what skills students need to develop. Materials are available in the classroom. These groups can also be flexible based on which students need help on any given day.

There are numerous benefits to incorporating a push-in model in the school. For younger students, for a pull-out-only model, the resource teacher must come to the class to get students who need help, resulting in a loss of instructional time. Furthermore, older students waste valuable instructional time during pull-out intervention by leaving the class to work with their remedial teacher in the resource room. Also, many students may not like to leave class for help out of fear of missing important work or feeling embarrassed. Finally, the remedial teacher faces a common challenge when the classroom teacher asks them to complete classwork. Because this work is often too challenging, it does not help students close the gap between their current reading level and the grade-level benchmark. In the push-in and pull-out model, the classroom and remedial teacher can build a stronger collaborative relationship, enabling them to discuss the student's reading level and strategies to help struggling readers close their reading gap.

By pairing the pull-out model with the push-in model, it's not either-or, but both-and. With the pull-out model, the student is removed from class and receives remedial help, usually in a resource room or center. The need for frequent support during the week is common for students who are significantly below grade level. With this model, they could receive push-in support during their language class and remedial help at another time in the day.

Accommodations

Accommodations refer to altering the learning or evaluation environment so that students who need extra support, regardless of whether they have an Individual Education Plan (IEP), have an equal chance of success or will not be disadvantaged by their limitations. In fact, in a study by David Scanlon and Diana Baker (2012), teachers interviewed about their experiences managing IEPs for their students stated that what they do for the students with an IEP is often beneficial to all students.

Classroom environmental accommodations can include extra textbooks for students who have difficulty remembering to bring their books to class, a copy of a classmate's or teacher's notes, or both oral and written instructions. Evaluation accommodations typically include extra time on tests and exams, using a computer to type rather than hand write responses, using assistive technology such as a reader or scribe, or taking the exam in a separate room. These accommodations in student participation, instructional delivery, or assessment do not reduce the criteria for success. For example, a student may receive additional time on an exam, but the success criteria would remain the same (Scanlon & Baker, 2012).

Most jurisdictions do not require a psychoeducational assessment for students to receive environmental or assessment accommodations. It is sufficient for a student to be identified as needing accommodations through in-house, curriculum-based assessments, such as DIBELS, Renaissance, or Aimsweb, parent and student input, and teacher observations. It is also important to experiment with various accommodations to determine if students are benefiting from them. To ensure the effective implementation of accommodations, Scanlon and Baker (2012) identify an effective three-step process that should be applied in K–12.

1. Prerequisites

2. Provisions

3. Evaluation of the plan and documentation in a student's IEP

Prerequisites

The prerequisite phase involves the clear identification of students' challenges and the accommodations they need to even the playing field.

For this first step, consider holding professional development sessions at the start of each year (and throughout the year if necessary) to help school staff understand the meaning of accommodations, the different types of accommodations, and the benefit of each accommodation to the success of the student. Schools should also ensure an effective and seamless process for transmitting data from elementary to middle and middle to high school. For example, middle schools need to ensure that students' elementary school information related to their accommodations is sent to the middle school.

Middle school teachers should also prepare students for the accommodations provided in high school to support their reading challenges. High school students with reading challenges, for example, often benefit from assistive technology for exams with extensive reading materials. However, I have observed that students do not usually use them, because to get used to accommodations like assistive technology to read exam questions, students need to use them for in-class tests throughout the year. Many students resist because they don't want to stand out among their peers. For some students, taking tests in another room is a more viable option. Also, for many students, the assistive technology is difficult to understand because the reader's tone sounds unnatural and is challenging to comprehend, especially without having enough practice (Boot, Owuor, Dinsmore, & MacLachlan, 2018; Kulkarni, Parmar, Selmi, & Mendleson, 2019; Shinohara & Wobbrock, 2011). For these reasons, it is essential that teachers prepare students for accommodations, explain their usefulness, and address challenges with the accommodations that might present themselves.

Ultimately, student agency is vitally important. Students need to feel empowered to choose the accommodations that will benefit them—and, therefore, they must be part of the decision-making process. Many problems can be resolved by explaining the benefits and offering a trial period, after which a further conversation can take place. For example, a student with a reading challenge may benefit from extra time as an accommodation. However, not all students with reading challenges need or benefit from having more time to complete an evaluation, especially if the student is provided with technology such as having the text read to them. It would be helpful to provide the student with extra time (the amount permitted often depends on the jurisdiction) and then ask if they found the extra time beneficial.

Provisions

The next stage in the process is provisions. This phase involves creating an organized list of all the students receiving accommodations. It includes each student's accommodations they received in elementary or middle school, with the additional accommodations that may be required to have in high school. Essential in this phase is to teach the student about their accommodations, why they are necessary, and how the student can advocate for them in the classroom. Classroom teachers are often unaware of the accommodations, which is often a source of frustration for parents. Students can learn about their accommodations and become effective advocates for themselves both in school and beyond. This might also include students' ability to explain the challenges they face resulting from the accommodation.

Updated lists of accommodations should be sent to all involved teachers. Teachers should keep these nearby to access regularly. For example, some schools put their IEP accommodations list on a Google Doc. That way, teachers can access the list quickly and make suggested changes. One list must remain unedited so teachers don't accidentally change allotted accommodations when making suggestions. Details can also be included, such as the type of accommodations needed, student resistance to the accommodations, and strategies that have been effectively applied to address the opposition. In this phase, it is also essential for teachers to recognize the fluid and flexible nature of accommodations. An accommodation that was required in an earlier grade may no longer be needed. Although typically students' accommodation needs don't often change much, it is important to recognize that they *might* change as students move up through the grades. Updated electronic lists of accommodations should be sent to all involved teachers.

Given the high number of students requiring accommodations to ensure students are on a level playing field, teachers may decide that instructional and evaluation methods will be incorporated into classroom practice. For example, extended time to write tests or assistive technology for a reader and a scribe can be built into the classroom structure. One way to address the extended time requirement is to build extra time into all class evaluations so they are available to those who need it. Those who finish early can receive in-class anchor activities to extend their learning. Also, to address the need for assistive technology, teachers across disciplines can ensure that all reading material and tests are uploaded onto students' laptops. Not all students should have a reader or scribe, but many environmental accommodations, like the accessible outline of notes, extra time as needed, and additional materials available in class, will be beneficial for many students.

Evaluation of the Plan and Documentation

The final phase in the process is evaluation. In this phase, teachers evaluate the environmental and assessment accommodations and additional accommodations. They continue effective supports, while those supports deemed ineffective or no longer necessary are stopped. In this process, high school students can take a leading role in identifying what supports were helpful and which were not (Scanlon & Baker, 2012).

Not all struggling readers will have or need an IEP, even though you may be providing accommodations for them. While schools should provide reading accommodations to all students, in most jurisdictions, evaluation accommodations such as an exam reader, a scribe, extended time, or writing the exam in a separate room must be documented on a student's IEP if they have one, especially at the high school and postsecondary levels. Other accommodations, such as an extra set of textbooks left in the classroom, one set of teacher's notes for the student, or a homework buddy are often included in the IEP for those who have one. This documentation is important so that teachers in the upcoming grades can continue to provide students with accommodations that have been shown to be beneficial. Finally, the IEP is only a document, a record of students' needs; unless implemented effectively, it is nothing more than a piece of paper. For students who have reading challenges, accommodations ensure that they can keep up with basic classroom requirements.

Table 4.1 (page 92) summarizes each of the support models this chapter explores, highlights the steps for implementation, and provides an example.

TABLE 4.1: Models for Support in Reading

STRATEGY AND EXPLANATION	THE STEPS	EXAMPLE
Acceleration: The acceleration model involves a series of steps to provide students at risk with the fundamental skills needed a few days before they are taught in the classroom.	**Step 1:** Present the student with a hook or an entry point related to the topic. **Step 2:** Establish learning goals and communicate these goals to the student. **Step 3:** Take a step back and fill in essential gaps. **Step 4:** Teach the student key vocabulary words necessary to engage in the new strategy. **Step 5:** Teach the new concept or skill. **Step 6:** Formatively assess the student.	How to identify metaphor in a text **Step 1:** The teacher reads a metaphorical text and asks students to draw a picture of what they just read. The teacher then explains that metaphors are often used to explain complex concepts and to bring text to life. **Step 2:** The teacher says, "By the end of our acceleration lesson, you will know what a metaphor is, the different types of metaphors used in a text, and how metaphors can help us understand written text. By the end of the lesson, you will be able to explain the meaning of the metaphor and how it helped you comprehend the passage." **Step 3:** The teacher reviews key grade-level vocabulary that students will need to know to read the text they will be working on during the acceleration lesson. **Step 4:** Teacher reviews the lesson's key vocabulary words such as figurative language and metaphor. Teacher provides students with words that will help identify a metaphor, such as *is*, *are*, and *were* and examples of metaphors. Finally, teacher gives students a list of steps to follow that includes (1) underline the words found in metaphors such as is, are, and were, (2) identify what is being compared (the sun to a ball of fire, the dog to a blanket, and so on), (3) identify the author's message or intention or why they used this metaphor, (4) note how the metaphor helped the student understand the author's message, and (5) summarize the passage. **Step 5:** Teacher provides a text with one or two metaphors. Teacher models the strategy by applying each of these steps. Then the teacher uses another text and practices the steps together with the students. Then students practice each of the strategies using another text, and then the students practice the steps on their own. **Step 6:** The teacher provides the student with a text and without guiding the student, he is asked to follow the steps to identify the meaning of the passage and how the metaphor is used to communicate the author's message.

STRATEGY AND EXPLANATION	THE STEPS	EXAMPLE
Anchor activities: Provide students who mastered the concept or skill with an alternative, advanced activity while other students complete the task or work with the teacher.	**Step 1:** All students work on the class activity. **Step 2:** Students who complete the in-class task work on an anchor activity independently. **Step 3:** Some students work on their own, completing the in-class task. **Step 4:** Students who need additional support to complete the classwork, work in a small group with the teacher. Imagine that the teacher has just taught specific graphemes in a phonics lesson or highlighted essential words in a vocabulary lesson. The teacher might introduce new strategies during the presentation and have students practice them through in-class activities. Students would likely fall into three groups: (1) Those who complete the activity quickly and are ready to move on, (2) students who need more time to complete the activity, and (3) students who need additional guidance from the classroom teacher. Students who complete the activity will be given an anchor activity and thus be occupied, enabling students who need more time to complete the task under less pressure. Those who require remedial support from the classroom teacher will receive it in a smaller group. Once the concept or strategy is clear, they can return to their seat and complete their work.	**Early elementary** **Step 1:** All students work on a reading activity involving letter-sound correspondence. **Step 2:** Students who complete the work on letter sounds work on an anchor activity creating a book of words associated with the sounds learned. **Step 3:** Other students use the time to complete the in-class activity. **Step 4:** Students who are unable to complete the in-class activity work with the teacher. **Middle elementary** **Step 1:** All students read a paragraph and identify the main ideas using the shrink the paragraph strategy. **Step 2:** Students who complete the task work on the anchor, which is to write out the steps to the shrink the paragraph strategy with images for each step that classmates can use. **Step 3:** Students work independently on completing the in-class assignment. **Step 4:** Students who are struggling work with the teacher. **Middle and high school** **Step 1:** Students are asked to read a complex expository text and identify the text pattern of each of the paragraphs or sections in the text (description, comparison, sequential, problem–solution). They are then asked to create a graphic organizer to represent each text pattern. **Step 2:** Students who complete this task correctly rewrite the text adding additional examples for each text pattern. For example, if one example is provided for the properties of acids and bases, students then provide one additional example and add it to their graphic organizer. **Step 3:** Students who are able to complete the task on their own but need more time continue to work on the task. **Step 4:** The teacher works with the students who are struggling. Once they are able to work on their own, they return to their seat and

continued →

STRATEGY AND EXPLANATION	THE STEPS	EXAMPLE
		(continued from previous page) continue working on the task. The teacher remains with the students who are struggling until they are able to complete the task on their own. Once the class ends, if students continue to have difficulty, they may need help during a lunch period.
Push-in and pull-out: Simultaneously provide push-in support in the classroom and pull-out support outside of the classroom.	**The push-in model:** The remedial teacher works with individual or small groups of students in the classroom during this time. The remaining students are working on independent work so the remedial teacher doesn't have to talk over the teacher's voice. The classroom teacher guides the resource teachers about what skills need to be developed. **The pull-out model:** Students work with the resource teacher outside of the classroom. Students can receive both push-in and pull-out support.	Following a reading lesson, students who need additional direct instruction work with the resource teacher in the classroom. The other students work on a task independently or with the support of the classroom teacher. These same students can receive remedial help at another time in the day as well to provide them with substantive support throughout the week.
Accommodations: Altering the learning or evaluation environment so that students who need extra support have an equal chance of success	**Step 1:** Prerequisites include professional development sessions at the start of each year for school staff to understand the meaning of accommodations, the different types of accommodations, and the benefit of each accommodation to the success of the student. **Step 2:** Provisions include creating an organized list of all the students receiving accommodations in elementary or middle school, and the accommodations that may be required in high school.	**Step 1:** Prerequisites Teachers receive training about environmental accommodations that include extra textbooks for students who have difficulty remembering to bring their books to class, a copy of a classmate's or teacher's notes, or both oral and written instructions. Evaluation accommodations typically include extra time on tests and exams, using a computer to type rather than hand write responses, assistive technology as a reader or scribe, or writing the exam in a separate room. **Step 2:** Provision Create a list in your school (typically the role of the resource teacher) of each student's accommodations.

STRATEGY AND EXPLANATION	THE STEPS	EXAMPLE
	(continued from previous page) **Step 3:** Evaluation and documentation where teachers evaluate the environment and accommodations. Effective supports are continued, and those deemed ineffective or no longer necessary are stopped. Older students take a leading role in identifying what supports were helpful and which were not.	*(continued from previous page)* **Step 3:** Evaluation Periodically throughout the year, evaluate the effectiveness of each student's accommodations. For example, a teacher may need to consult with the student about having additional time to write tests, if, for example, the student hasn't used the extra time on the past five evaluations, or the student may request not to use automated text such as Word Q as it is not helping him understand the questions in an evaluation.

Conclusion

Many different models and approaches are needed to ensure that students receive evidence-based reading instruction. This chapter presented a variety of models suited to providing support to students with learning gaps in reading: acceleration, anchor activities, push-in and pull-out, and accommodations. Perfection should not be the goal in implementing these models—jumping in and trying and then evaluating the results is a great start.

The next chapter addresses reading instruction across the content areas.

Models of Reading Support: Next Steps

Strategy	How I will implement the strategy	Reflections
Acceleration		
Anchor Activities		
Push-in and Pull-out		
Accommodations		

CHAPTER 5

READING INSTRUCTION ACROSS CONTENT AREAS

Several years ago, I worked with a student who was a proficient decoder. Throughout elementary school, his teachers assumed he was well on his way to becoming a proficient comprehender. However, he began to struggle in middle school, and his grades plummeted. Despite being a skilled decoder, he had not learned how to comprehend text, especially fact-based text, which is more common in middle and high school. It became apparent upon looking more closely at his Universal Screening Assessment that his comprehension skills were underdeveloped. He needed to learn how to comprehend fact-based texts across all content areas.

As discussed throughout this book, reading development is the gateway to academic success in elementary, middle school, high school, college, and beyond. Students who struggle to read and comprehend text will miss out on many opportunities that they would otherwise have. Importantly, students shouldn't struggle with reading skills because we know from the research that reading can be taught and learned as long as instruction follows a trajectory of reading development (the big 5 of literacy; Klages, Scholtens, Fowler, & Frierson, 2020).

This chapter presents specific strategies content-area teachers can use to boost reading proficiency to assist students in their comprehension of content-area text.

All Teachers Are Reading Teachers

While content teachers (science, history, mathematics, and so on) should not feel responsible for teaching students to decode text, their students will not be successful in their content classes without having mastered basic reading skills (McNorgan,

2021). Students' success in these classes requires reading proficiency so they can comprehend the content-area text and discipline-area advanced content. Content-area teachers should be mindful of the strategies necessary to teach discipline-specific content; in addition, they should be on the lookout for students who have not attained fundamental reading skills. All teachers need to be advocates for students who are struggling.

According to the most recent evaluation data from the Programme for International Student Assessment (PISA, 2018), nearly one in five fifteen-year-olds scored below the lowest proficiency level in literacy, which the Organisation for Economic Co-operation and Development (OECD) defines as "students' capacity to understand, use, evaluate, reflect on, and engage with texts to achieve one's goals; develop one's knowledge and potential; and participate in society" (as cited in PISA, 2018).

Alan Armstrong (2015), the past president of the Consortium of Institutions for the Development of Education and Research in Europe, poses two critical questions for teaching literacy across the curriculum.

First, Armstrong (2015) asks, in a fast-changing world of social media, video games, constant advertising, and more: "How can teachers work together most effectively to prepare learners for the literacy skills they will need to access their learning across the curriculum now?" (p. 5).

Second, Armstrong (2015) asks, "How can [teachers across the curriculum] promote a sufficiently deep understanding and enjoyment of literacy that will ensure [students] continue to develop such skills actively throughout their lives?" (p. 5).

According to Vicki Urquhuart and Dana Frazee (2012), teachers deserve to have "research-based answers to their overarching questions about teaching reading in the content areas" (p. xviii). This chapter answers these questions by identifying the strategies that enable students to become proficient readers in all content areas.

Challenges in Content-Area Reading

Despite the best efforts of classroom teachers and special educators, many students struggle in the content-area courses. Furthermore, according to the National Assessment of Educational Progress (2022), only 36 percent of fourth graders and 26 percent of eighth graders are proficient readers, a slight decline since the pre-COVID-19 assessment conducted in 2019. However, most concerning is that the lowest 10 percent of readers suffered the most significantly since 2019, and the highest 90th percentile suffered the least. Teachers often hear from these students that the work is too difficult or boring (Urquhuart & Frazee, 2012). Students who struggle in school are often labeled as learning disabled, unmotivated, or even lazy when many have given up because they have come to believe that there is a skill critical to school success that they cannot master.

The challenge content-area teachers face is that many students who experience difficulty in content courses lack the comprehension skills to "mentally organize" content in each discipline (Shanahan & Shanahan, 2008). Furthermore, while content-area teachers have a lot of content knowledge, they may lack the literacy skills to teach students to comprehend text in their discipline. Literacy experts, who have specific knowledge about how to teach comprehension, especially to struggling students, may lack the content knowledge to guide content-area teachers. Ultimately, special educators and language specialists need to learn more about specific skills needed in each content area so content-area teachers can incorporate these strategies within their instructional repertoire.

Strategies for Reading Success in the Content Areas

Students need to learn two types of strategies for successful reading in the content areas: (1) generic reading strategies, which are helpful throughout all disciplines, and (2) discipline-specific strategies.

Generic Comprehension Strategies

Generic comprehension strategies—strategies that can be used across disciplines—typically address the processes required before, during, and after reading if students are to comprehend subject-matter texts. *Pre-reading strategies* provide students with context and background information about the content; the more students know about the subject matter, the more likely they will be to use that context to understand what they are reading. *During-the-reading strategies* encourage the reader to engage in active reading and monitor their comprehension as they read. *Post-reading techniques* enable the reader to connect the text to their own experiences (Graesser, Cai et al., 2016). Marcia Kosanovich, Deborah Reed, and Debra Miller (2010) offer five research-based recommendations for content-area teachers to help students be proficient nonfiction readers.

1. Provide explicit instruction and supportive, modeled practice.

2. Increase the amount of teacher-led and student-focused discussion about the content.

3. Set and maintain high standards in all areas of literacy.

4. Increase students' motivation.

5. Teach essential content knowledge.

Table 5.1 summarizes these recommendations.

TABLE 5.1: Recommendations to Increase Comprehension Skills Across Content Areas

RECOMMENDATIONS	EXPLANATION
1. Provide explicit teaching and supportive practice.	Teach students when and how to apply strategies, such as graphic organizers and questioning techniques, and provide students with many opportunities to use effective strategies and receive feedback. Apply gradual release of responsibility using the *I do, we do, you do one, you do many* approach to explicit teaching. (See Chapter 2, page 21, for more details on this approach.) Encourage students to become aware of their cognitive processes of constructing meaning when attempting to comprehend text.
2. Increase opportunities for teacher-led and student-focused discussion about the content.	Prompt students with questions about the text and encourage students to speak with one another in small groups to think critically about the text.
3. Set high standards for students' comprehension of text.	Use evidence-based practices that facilitate students' comprehension such as shrink the paragraph (page 51) and reciprocal teaching (page 55). Teachers must believe that with effective instructional approaches, all students can reach a high level of comprehension.
4. Increase student motivation.	Increase students' engagement with the text. Provide students with text options and assignments. Increase students' interaction with one another. Share learning goals with students and ensure they have exemplars of success.
5. Teach content knowledge.	Focus on content knowledge or knowledge in each discipline, and teach vocabulary, concepts, and facts relevant to each field.

Additional generic strategies include the preparation, assistance, and reflection (PAR) strategy (Ortlieb & Cheek, 2013), text structures, frontloading vocabulary, using guiding questions during reading, using active reading strategies, visualizing, making connections, multimodal representation, and three-level readings of the text.

The PAR Strategy

The *prepare, assistance, and reflection (PAR) strategy* (Ortlieb & Cheek, 2013) highlights the need to prepare students to read a text, use assistance strategies during reading, and implement reflection strategies post-reading. Preparation strategies include motivational approaches to arouse students' curiosity about the text, such as posing questions, making connections to students' background knowledge, predicting what the text is about, and addressing text problems that may arise during reading. Teachers should encourage students to ask themselves questions such as, *What do I already know about the text?*, *What do I predict the text may be about?*, and *What can I preview before reading the text, such as the graphs, tables, pictures, or headings?*

The assistance phase includes teaching students how to self-monitor to understand and connect to the text. Asking questions while you read a text is an excellent way to check for understanding. For example, if a science text begins with "Mitosis is an important part of cell division that helps organisms grow and repair themselves" (Let's Talk Science, 2019), the student would be taught to stop and ask themselves a question such as, *What is the purpose of mitosis?* Additionally, students should be taught to reread the text, write notes as they read, review their predictions, and search for connections. Figure 5.1 presents a template students can use to remind themselves to ask these essential questions while reading their text.

Questions	Student Responses
After my first reading of the text, what are the key ideas?	
After rereading the text, would I add anything to my summary of key ideas?	
After reading the passage, what image do I have of the text?	
After reading the text, can I confirm or reject my predictions?	
What comes to mind as I read the text? What does the text or text passage remind me of?	

FIGURE 5.1: During reading questions.

Visit **go.SolutionTree.com/literacy** *to download the free reproducible version of this figure.*

Finally, the reflective phase should take place after reading and includes talking and writing opportunities to assess students' understanding of the material. For example, students can partner with another student and speak about their summary of the passage, discuss their predictions, and respond to or write critical questions starting with a few of these question prompts: How many?, Which one?, Why did?, Why would?, How did?, Which did?, or When did?

Text Structures

Another generic strategy is teaching students expository text structures such as (1) description/attribution, (2) compare and contrast, (3) cause and effect, (4) problem/solution, and (5) sequential and chronological. Begin by teaching students each text structure, one at a time, highlighting the keywords (cue words) common to that text structure. Next, present students with a graphic organizer they can use to represent the structure visually. When practicing, students should master one text structure at a time, collecting the information with each structure and representing it using the graphic organizer. Once students have learned each structure individually, they can use a text with multiple text structures to practice identifying the text structure using critical vocabulary and then visually represent it using the appropriate structure. Figure 5.2 presents five text structures, their cue words, and the appropriate graphic organizer.

Additionally, this is an excellent study technique because it facilitates students' ability to identify the essential information in the passage. Reviewing the information on the graphic organizer is often more accessible, especially for students with poor reading skills, because studying a visual image is more manageable than rereading the entire passage.

Frontloading Vocabulary

According to Ortlieb and Cheek (2013), for students to read a text, they need to understand at least 90 percent of the vocabulary. Therefore, content-area teachers should teach challenging vocabulary before students are expected to read the text. According to Margarita Espino Calderón and Shawn Slakk (2018), preteaching vocabulary is especially useful for second language learners, but it is a strategy that should be used for all learners.

Pattern	Description	Cue Words (Signal Words)	Graphic Organizer
Description	The author describes a topic by listing characteristics, features, attributes, and examples.	• for example • characteristics • for instance • such as • is like • including • to illustrate	
Sequence	The author lists items or events in numerical or chronological sequence, either explicit or implied.	• first • second • third • later • next • before • then • finally • after • when • later • since • now • previously • actual use of dates	
Comparison	Information is presented by detailing how two or more events, concepts, theories, or things are alike or different.	• however • nevertheless • on the other hand • but • similarly • although • also • in contrast • different • alike • same as • either/or • in the same way • just like • just as • likewise • in comparison • whereas • yet	

continued →

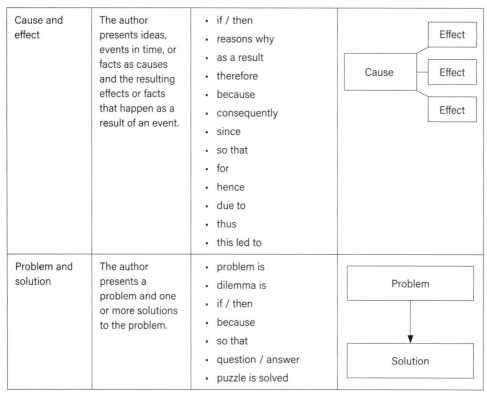

Cause and effect	The author presents ideas, events in time, or facts as causes and the resulting effects or facts that happen as a result of an event.	• if / then • reasons why • as a result • therefore • because • consequently • since • so that • for • hence • due to • thus • this led to	
Problem and solution	The author presents a problem and one or more solutions to the problem.	• problem is • dilemma is • if / then • because • so that • question / answer • puzzle is solved	

Source: Adapted from Colorado Education Initiative, n.d.

FIGURE 5.2: Five expository text structures, their word cues, and graphic organizers.

*Visit **go.SolutionTree.com/literacy** to download the free reproducible version of this figure.*

The importance of frontloading vocabulary is exemplified in the following text example.

> "Strange Bedfellows!" lamented the title of a recent letter to *Museum News*, in which a certain Harriet Sherman excoriated the National Gallery of Art in Washington for its handling of tickets to the much-ballyhooed "Van Gogh's van Goghs" exhibit. A huge proportion of the 200,000 free tickets were snatched up by the opportunists in the dead of winter, who then scalped those tickets at $85 apiece to less hardy connoisseurs. (Kaplan Test Prep, n.d., para. 2)

By briefly telling students the context (a woman who wrote an article in a newspaper to express dissatisfaction) and teaching the difficult words, such as *bedfellows* (people with whom you are familiar) *lamented* (expressing unhappiness), *excoriated* (harshly criticized) *ballyhooed* (exaggerated speech), *opportunists* (those who take advantage of an opportunity), and *connoisseurs* (people who know a lot about a subject such as art), students will be able to understand what they're reading.

Students need to use context to comprehend difficult words, but if too many words are unknown to the reader, they won't be able to make use of the context to decipher the unfamiliar words. It may be best for students to read a text at the appropriate vocabulary level so most words are familiar, but especially in high school where texts are often mandatory, the option to provide different-level texts to students based on their vocabulary or comprehension level may not be available.

The tea party strategy is an effective and fun way for elementary, middle, and high school students to learn essential words in a text before reading it (Beers, 2003). First, teachers identify no more than twenty challenging words in the text and add them to a table like the one in figure 5.3. All students receive a paper copy of the word chart with a different word defined on each student's copy (see figure 5.3). Students then circulate around the classroom in tea party fashion, sharing the definition of their word with one student at a time and writing down the meaning of each student's word. Once students have the written definition of all the words, they sit in groups of four and discuss their text predictions orally using the new words. For example, a summary could be, "I think the text will be about the need to abolish a law in a particular country. The people will be happy about this decision because the policy is harsh. The people threatened to revolt if the policy wasn't abolished." The last step is for students to write down their predictions individually.

Words	Definition
Abolish	
Memorable	
Harsh	Cruel or severe
Revolt	

FIGURE 5.3: Sample tea party list of words and definitions.

*Visit **go.SolutionTree.com/literacy** to download the free reproducible version of this figure.*

Guiding Questions

While reading, students should continuously ask themselves questions about what they read. This strategy serves as a form of self-checking. If they can answer the questions, they should continue reading, but if not, they should reread the text (Ortlieb & Cheek, 2013). Using the earlier example, in a text that reads "Mitosis is an important part of cell division that helps organisms grow and repair themselves" (Let's Talk

Science, 2019), a self-checking question could be, *What is the purpose of mitosis?* In addition to asking specific questions about the text as they read, students should also have questions in mind that they ask themselves continuously (McKnight, 2014). Some questions to ask are, *What is the author telling me?*, *Why is it an important concept or fact?*, and *What else do I know about this information?*

Active Reading Strategies

Reading in the content areas requires active reading and engagement with the text. However, much of the instruction around active reading eludes students and often becomes the hidden curriculum—skills known to the high achievers but unknown to those who struggle. Therefore, students need to be taught specific strategies that enable them to actively and dynamically interact with the text. Equally important is that students have a purpose when reading a text. One approach is called *plus, minus, interesting (PMI)*, developed by de Bono (1985) in his work on critical thinking. While reading an expository text, guide students to think about what they agree with (plus), what they disagree with (minus), and a point that they find interesting. For example, you can provide students with a written text of presidential speeches and ask them to highlight the plus, minus, and interesting points in the text (see figure 5.4).

Text from a Franklin D. Roosevelt speech, March 12, 1933:

This is a day of national consecration. And I am certain that on this day my fellow Americans expect that on my induction into the Presidency I will address them with a candor and a decision which the present situation of our people impels. This is preeminently the time to speak the truth, the whole truth, frankly and boldly. Nor need we shrink from honestly facing conditions in our country today. This great Nation will endure as it has endured, will revive and will prosper. So, first of all, let me assert my firm belief that the only thing we have to fear is fear itself—nameless, unreasoning, unjustified terror which paralyzes needed efforts to convert retreat into advance. In every dark hour of our national life a leadership of frankness and vigor has met with that understanding and support of the people themselves which is essential to victory. I am convinced that you will again give that support to leadership in these critical days. (Roosevelt, 1933)

P: plus (or positive)	That he is addressing the people with honesty
M: minus (or negative)	That the country is in a bad situation
I: interesting	That he says the only thing you have to fear is fear itself

FIGURE 5.4: PMI strategy example.

*Visit **go.SolutionTree.com/literacy** to download the free reproducible version of this figure.*

Fact-question-response (FQR) is another active learning strategy that supports active learning of expository text (Harvey & Goudvis, 2007). Give students a grade-level text and blue, pink, and yellow self-stick notes (or colored self-stick arrows).

Instruct students to place the blue notes next to the factual information in the text (for example, dolphins are mammals), the pink notes for confusing passages or difficult words requiring further information (for example, dolphins are cetaceans), and the yellow notes next to the passage that helps to clarify the problematic text (for example, cetaceans are mammals such as whales and dolphins that live in water and whose bodies have been adapted for this life such as having flippers).

Active learning can also involve providing students with an advanced organizer chart, as shown in figure 5.5, that they can complete as they read a text. The advanced organizer can go a long way toward indicating to students what to look for in a text and helping them remain active as they read the text.

Habitats	Climate	Animals that live there	Adaptation (Unique features of the animal that allow it to survive in that habitat)
Forest			
Grassland			
Wetlands			
Desert			

FIGURE 5.5: Advanced organizer for a text on animal habitats.

*Visit **go.SolutionTree.com/literacy** to download the free reproducible version of this figure.*

Another similar strategy is annotating text (Wilfong, 2019), which acts as a way for the reader to interact (converse) with the text as they read; better yet, have a conversation with the author. For example, as students are reading a text, they may note that they are now reading a heading or subheading and think to themselves, "The author is introducing me to a new idea." They would then use an annotation to identify it as a subheading. As they continue reading, they may come upon an important word and note that word using a specific annotation for key content vocabulary. According to Lori Wilfong (2019), this strategy helps make readers' internal discussions external. Additionally, annotating helps students slow down and prevent the mind from wandering or daydreaming while reading. Table 5.2 shows the actions and symbols readers use to annotate text.

TABLE 5.2: Actions and Symbols to Annotate Text

TEXT	ACTION TAKEN BY READER	SYMBOL
Headings and subheadings	Circle	◯
Key content vocabulary	Box	▭
Other difficult words	Triangle	△
Important facts or main ideas	Double underline	═══
Supporting evidence for facts or main ideas	Single underline	───
Procedural words	Arrow	⇨
Confusing information	Question mark	?
Major conclusion drawn	Star	☆

Source: Adapted from Wilfong, 2019.

Visualizing

Another helpful strategy while reading is visualizing the text. According to Ellin Oliver Keene and Susan Zimmerman, "Proficient readers spontaneously and purposely create mental images while and after they read. The images emerge from all five senses as well as the emotions and are anchored in a reader's prior knowledge" (Keene & Zimmermann, 2007, p. 196). Visualizing is more difficult for some students than others; therefore, guiding students so they can picture texts is essential.

The best way to support students is to ask them questions to enhance visualization. Teachers first ask general questions to elicit visualization and, if necessary, go deeper and ask more specific and guided questions. For example, a visualizing prompt could be, *What do you see when you read the passage?* A more direct question could be, *What are the animals doing?* The questions are not based on students' comprehension of the text because the questions do not directly respond to information presented in the text. However, while reading, visual images should emerge and help the student hold onto essential information.

Visualizing can also take the form of pictures that can help readers organize and recall information. For example, when reading about a process that involves nine steps, students could imagine a train with nine cars, and on each car is a picture of each step (Leighton Gamel, 2015).

Making Predictions

According to Amy Alexandra Wilson and Kathryn Chavez (2014), students can begin to predict what they think the text is about using background knowledge and text features such as titles, headings, subheadings, images, and tables. Additionally, students can use text features such as headings to help them understand the content during reading. For example, the header might indicate that the upcoming passage focuses on cause and effect.

According to Amy Leighton Gamel (2015), providing students with an outline that includes predictions and purpose is beneficial. Teachers could give students a worksheet that consists of the title of the chapter and predictions that students could make based on the title, headings, subheadings, images, figures, graphs, and all other visual information. Additionally, Leighton Gamel (2015) suggests including purpose as a prompt on the worksheet, asking students what they might want to learn in this chapter based on the identified information.

Making Connections

To fully comprehend text, readers must form mental representations; to do this, they must be able to integrate what they already know and what they are currently learning. Therefore, it is essential to offer guided practice in connecting knowledge to prior readings, earlier passages students already read in their current text, or using their background knowledge related to their experiences or connections to events (McMaster, Espin, & van den Broek, 2014). Given the critical role of background knowledge in facilitating comprehension, teaching students how to access their background knowledge while reading is necessary (Wilson & Chavez, 2014). Students can ask themselves questions such as, *What does this text remind me of?*, *How does this passage connect to the passage I just read?*, *Have I read a similar book?*, and *Does this relate to a world event?*

Multimodal Presentations of Text

Another excellent strategy to ensure deep learning of text is instructing students to create representations of what they read using a different format (Wilson & Chavez, 2014). For example, a student could be asked to convert a mathematical equation to an image. In social studies, students could be asked to transform a picture into an infographic. The idea here is that students transform the written text into either a format of their choice or one identified by their teacher. Examples of options for different modes of presentation of a text are pictures, graphic organizers, timelines, video clips, infographics, PowerPoint presentations, speeches, or dialogues.

Three-Level Guides

This strategy requires students to read the text three times, each time with a different purpose (Ortlieb & Cheek, 2013). The first reading, level 1, involves reading the text while focusing on factual information. Students can ask themselves questions starting with prompts such as *What happened?, How many?, How did?, Who did?,* or *What is the definition?* The second reading, level 2, is interpretive and requires students to read between the lines. Students can ask themselves questions that begin with prompts such as *Why did?, What was?,* or *Can you explain?* Finally, level 3 involves reading beyond the lines and requires generalizations, comparisons, and judgments. Questions such as *What would have happened if?, Do you agree?,* or *How might?* help students begin to move away from the literal meaning of the text and infer information not directly in the text. With these specific questions, the students can begin to move away from the literal meaning of texts and make assumptions based on the information. High-level comprehension requires this skill of inferring because information often needs to be interpreted beyond its literal meaning in order to fully comprehend the text.

Discipline-Specific Strategies

Discipline-specific strategies relate to how information is structured in each domain or subject area. Perhaps most important, students must master discipline-specific language to comprehend discipline-specific texts fully. According to Kristi Santi and Deborah Reed (2015), disciplinary texts, especially social studies and science texts at the high school level, have many specialized vocabulary words with high levels of linguistic difficulty. Readers need to know about 90 percent of words to comprehend a text; thus, knowledge of these specialized words will significantly impact students' comprehension.

Additionally, students need twelve to twenty-five exposures to a word to become proficient and able to use it, define it, and have it become part of their vocabulary (Lupo, Hardigree, Thacker, Sawyer, & Merritt, 2022). Teachers should encourage students to speak about the content area using discipline-specific terms and their meanings. For example, students should discuss mathematics problems using mathematics language. For example, students should be encouraged to use words such as *quotient*, the sum when dividing numbers, rather than non-mathematics language such as *the answer*. In social studies, students should be encouraged to use historical language such as *nomad* instead of a more generic word like *wanderer*.

To become proficient with terminology across multiple contexts, students need to do what is referred to as wide reading (Lupo et al., 2022). *Wide reading* means reading books from various contexts and genres because words have different meanings depending on the context. For example, a *solution* in social science implies a solution to a problem, whereas in science, a *solution* refers to a solvent with a substance dissolved in it. A *translation* in mathematics refers to the movement of an object from one place to another or a "geometric transformation" (Venema, 2006). A *translation* in other disciplines takes on a different meaning, such as translating vocabulary from one language to another (Lupo et al., 2022). Because vocabulary can mean something different across contexts, discipline-specific vocabulary needs to be taught and learned.

Mathematics

To solve mathematics problems, students need reading comprehension skills specific to mathematics (Boonen, de Koning, Jolles, & van der Schoot, 2016) and knowledge of specific mathematics vocabulary. First, teachers need to teach mathematics representation skills. These are the skills that require students to transform the word situation (what needs to be solved), often hidden in the word problem, into a mental representation. Creating this mental representation, which could include drawing tables, figures, number lines, or models such as with fractions, enables students to develop a plan to solve the problem (Kemp, 2010). This skill is challenging for some students as they typically address an impulsive response and focus only on the superficial numbers presented without fully understanding the problem the text presents (Boonen et al., 2016). For this reason, it is essential to provide students with time to examine the problem and visually represent it without the immediate pressure of having to solve it (Kemp, 2010).

Second, successful reading comprehension requires students to respond to the word problem's specific semantic elements, such as the elements in the problem that are known and unknown (Boonen et al., 2016). Given the unique comprehension features of mathematics word problems, these skills must be taught explicitly. Teachers could help students by modeling the steps to effective problem solving, beginning with mental representations.

Third, mathematics problems using language are, by and large, an assessment of students' reading ability and language skills. Learning the language of mathematics may be like learning a new language. Therefore, students must have a solid foundation of mathematics terms such as *circumference, polynomial,* and *quotient,* to name a few (Ortlieb & Cheek, 2013), and explicit instruction in mathematics vocabulary is essential (Avalos, Bengochea, & Secada, 2015). Mary Avalos, Alain Bengochea, and Walter Secada (2015) cite research indicating that many mathematics teachers may resist teaching vocabulary because it is perceived as being out of the scope of their discipline. However, it is difficult to comprehend the problem without access to the meaning of the words. Furthermore, vocabulary instruction must go beyond the superficial meaning of terms, enabling students to comprehend the vocabulary within the context of mathematics.

According to authors Sarah Lupo, Christine Hardigree, Emma Thacker, Amanda Sawyer, and Joi Meritt (2022), teachers often mistakenly ask students to look for keywords to help them solve problems. For example, students may be told that if the problem has the phrase *in all,* the operation is addition. However, as they point out in a clear example, using this strategy can be misleading. Their example states, "Meredith had 6 puppies. She gave some puppies to Carrie. Then, she had 4 puppies left. How many puppies in all did Meredith give to Carrie?" (Lupo et al., 2022). The operation here is subtraction, but if students use keywords to indicate the operation, they would mistakenly believe that the operation needed to complete the problem is addition. Rather than focus on keywords as an indication of the operation required, students should be taught to create their representation of the problem. According to Kristin Kemp (2010), to be a successful problem solver, students need to learn both concepts and procedures. Therefore, in addition to deep learning of the concept (such as fractions or integers), students also need to learn the procedure or steps to follow. Teachers should follow an explicit teaching approach to teaching students procedures, such as the I do, we do, you do one, and you do many approach (see chapter 2, page 21, for details). The steps they should follow could be (1) read the problem, (2) read the problem a second time, (3) create a picture of the problem using either a drawing or manipulatives, (4) write down the operation, (5) solve the problem, and (6) revisit the problem to analyze if you have correctly captured the identified problem.

A final note that is important to all disciplines, but perhaps most relevant in mathematics, is the importance of avoiding cognitive overload. *Cognitive overload* occurs when too many concepts are presented simultaneously (de Jong, 2010). Therefore, mathematics teachers should identify the lesson's focus and teach mastery of one concept at a time. For example, if teachers present mathematics problems with unknown results, such as "Laura had ten dolls. Her sister gave her two more dolls for her birthday. How many dolls did she have then?" (Lupo et al., 2022, p. 165), they should allow students to work toward mastery before introducing a new kind of problem. Once mastered, students could work on problems with a start unknown such as "Laura had some dolls. Her sister gave her two more dolls for her birthday. Then, she had 12 dolls. How many dolls did Laura have before her birthday?" (Lupo et al., 2022, p. 165). The importance of teaching one concept or problem type at a time and teaching it to mastery before presenting a second type cannot be overemphasized.

Social Studies

Critiques of history education in the K–12 classroom have focused mainly on a lack of understanding of history as a discipline and how historians approach their profession (Massey, 2015). To examine this notion, researchers who have tried to explore how historians approach the field are primarily focused on inquiry methods rather than on what currently exists in many middle school, high school, and college classrooms—viewing history as a form of memorization whereby students need to amass a list of dates related to events that occurred. "Doing history," as Dixie D. Massey (2015, p. 23) identifies it, is mainly about reading and making sense of historical texts (VanSledright, 2004, as cited in Massey, 2015). Therefore, to become an effective comprehender in the social sciences, particularly in history, students need to become adept at the inquiry and interpretation methods of comprehension. Additionally, historical texts have been scrutinized because they give students the impression that information is factual rather than interpretive, specifically concerning causes that led to critical events. For this reason, teachers should include primary sources and other texts so that middle and high school readers can more deeply understand history as a discipline that involves examining and interpreting texts (Massey, 2015).

In particular, current genres in many middle and high school classrooms include written documents such as diaries and letters or government documents, newspapers and magazine articles, maps, and photographs, and each genre has its own text pattern (Massey, 2015).

One effective strategy to make sense of historical documents is the *SCIM-C strategy* (Hicks, Doolittle, & Ewing, 2004). The acronym stands for *summarizing, contextualizing, inferring, monitoring,* and *corroborating.* During the summarizing stage, students read the document and identify some essential elements by asking questions such as, *What type of document is it?, What do you know about the document (date, title, author)?, What specific information is provided in the document?, Who is the intended audience?,* and *What is the message the document transmits?*

The contextualizing stage involves information such as who produced the document, when and why it was written (what was its intended goal), and what was happening locally when the document was created. Also, students should ask questions such as, *How reliable is the source?* The inferring stage asks students to identify what conclusions they might draw from the document, any biases inherent in the document, and if there is information about the context of the document. The monitoring stage involves any missing information from the document and if there is information that requires further study.

Finally, the corroborating stage involves asking the student to find other documents that relate to this one—what might be other sources that either confirm or reject the information stated in the document? See table 5.3 for specific questions that students can ask at each stage of the SCIM-C process (Hicks, Doolittle, & Ewing, 2004).

TABLE 5.3: A Summary of the SCIM-C Strategy

ELEMENTS OF THE SCIM-C STRATEGY	QUESTIONS TO ASK	EXAMPLE
Summarizing	What type of document is this? What perspective is provided in this document? Why was this document written? Who wrote the document?	A fifteen-year-old boy wrote a letter addressed to the Department of Labor. The boy is asking for help so he can continue his schooling.
Contextualizing	When was the document written? What historical question is intended to be answered by the document? What was happening historically during the time the document was written?	The document was written in 1939 (ten years after the depression), but life was still difficult for this boy who lived in Arkansas. The boy is seeking financial assistance from the government because many of his family members died—and a single mother is raising him.

Inferring	What points of view are presented in the document? Is there anything omitted from the document that should have been included?	Although this boy is fifteen, he is mature, and he wants to ensure that his schooling does not negatively impact his family. He is worried about his mother. The boy does not speak about what happened to the rest of his family.
Monitoring	What other information is needed to understand the context of the document fully? What images, ideas, or terms need to be more fully explained?	Was there something specific about his experience during the depression that is important to know? What happened to his family members? Why was education so important to this fifteen-year-old? What else can we learn about his town that might help with the overall context of the letter?
Corroborating	Is this document similar to other sources or documents you have seen? What additional sources are needed to fully understand the context and message in this document?	I read a letter from someone similar to this one, but that took place in another part of the United States. I would like to learn more about what life was like in 1939 in this town. Were they aware that it was the start of WW2?

Source: Hicks, Doolittle, & Ewing 2004.

Another challenge for students is the specialized vocabulary required to comprehend a historical text. Students will encounter more than six hundred discipline-specific words in a text (Bailey, 2007). Furthermore, many of these words are archaic and, while no longer used in modern-day discourse, are still required to comprehend historical texts (Moje, Stockdill, Kim, & Kim, 2011). One example of this comes from Bill Bryson (1990), "Brave once implied cowardice—as indeed bravado still does" (p. 77). Therefore, teachers need to teach vocabulary explicitly, teaching words essential to comprehending a social science text. As mentioned in the generic strategies section, frontloading vocabulary using the tea party strategy can be beneficial here. Middle and high school teachers can work together to identify essential vocabulary needed to comprehend social studies text at each grade level and then teach the vocabulary explicitly using a Frayer diagram, such as the one shown in figure 5.6 (Frayer et al., 1969, page 116).

Point of view is equally important and often challenging for students. Texts can present multiple perspectives; thus, students need to learn how to interpret points of view. First, students need to be instructed to focus on whose point of view is presented. Then, they need to have time to examine how that individual or group's point of view might be influencing their historical perspective. Examine Both Sides (EBS)

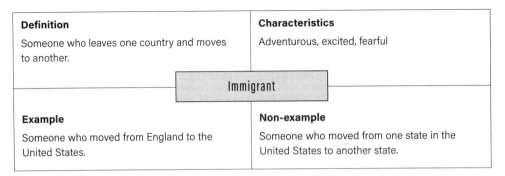

Definition	Characteristics
Someone who leaves one country and moves to another.	Adventurous, excited, fearful

Immigrant

Example	Non-example
Someone who moved from England to the United States.	Someone who moved from one state in the United States to another state.

FIGURE 5.6: Example of a Frayer diagram.

*Visit **go.SolutionTree.com/literacy** to download the free reproducible version of this figure.*

is a good strategy that enables students to focus on multiple points of view related to historical events. For example, while reading a document on the Vietnam War, students can ask themselves questions such as: *Who is writing the document?*, *What evidence do you have of this?*, and *What passages in the document indicate a person or a group's viewpoint?* Students can then be asked to look at the article from the perspective of another person or group, how they might respond to it, and what would be different if that group were writing the text.

Fact versus opinion is another challenging dimension of social studies texts that should be taught as a concept before layering it with content. Students need to first learn fact versus opinion using content familiar to them; for example, how many siblings I have (fact) versus my brother is a nice person (opinion). Questions such as, *Can it be proven, observed, or is it a person's feeling, thought, or judgment?* help students question whether the information is factual or opinion-based (Ortlieb & Cheek, 2013).

Finally, all social science texts of either a narrative or expository nature are built around a text structure. For example, diaries may be more narrative in design, with story elements such as character and setting, initiating events, problems, and solutions. Magazine articles or textbooks may be descriptive or sequential or involve cause-and-effect text patterns. To master these diverse texts successfully, students must learn to identify text patterns. A descriptive text pattern might be around the attributes of the Treaty of Versailles, such as: "The Treaty outlined the conditions for peace between Germany and the Allies. It was led by the United States, France, and the United Kingdom. It placed blame on Germany and other powers for the war and led to significant reparations" (National Geographic, n.d.).

Additionally, the sequence of events in social studies, particularly in historical texts, is critical to students' comprehension in this discipline. Often presented as a timeline, this type of representation requires students to recall a lot of information that could appear rote or disconnected from context, thus challenging the student's working memory. Therefore, students need to be able to identify sequential text structures when reading them in their textbooks. Using our example of the Treaty of Versailles, a passage of text may present the sequence of events as follows: (1) January 8, 1917, Woodrow Wilson presents an outline of his fourteen points required to reach peace between Germany and the allies; (2) November 11, 1918, German leaders signed the armistice peace treaty; (3) January 18, 1919, the Paris conference took place; and (4) the Treaty was signed on June 28, 1919.

Another challenge is identifying cause and effect in the text and understanding the causal relationship. This text pattern is particularly challenging in social science texts when there are multiple causes, such as the causes and consequences of World War II. For example, the causes could be written in a text as the impact of the Treaty of Versailles, the economic depression, the rise of fascism in Germany and other countries, and failure of the League of Nations, which led to the consequence of a six-year war (Drishti IAS, 2020).

Social science texts are also rife with comparisons and contrasts. A text may compare the Treaty of Versailles to the Treaty of Saint-Germain-en-Laye regarding the goal, results, and countries implicated. However, students need to learn how to compare and contrast as a skill before they can compare and contrast content-rich information. I suggest teaching students the skill of comparison with content they are familiar with—comparing themselves to their siblings, food they like to food they dislike, their neighborhood to another neighborhood, and one movie to another. Once they master the skill of comparison with familiar content, they can transfer the skill (with guidance and scaffolding) to newly learned content. Deep learning of text structures can benefit students during assessments as many questions are based on one of the particular text structures requiring students to compare or describe events or leaders, list causes or consequences, or recall a series of events.

Adequate comprehension of historical texts requires explicit teaching of strategies and the time to practice these strategies and engage in further research when necessary. This is impossible when the focus is on memorizing dates and events for a high-stakes evaluation. School systems need to decide if the focus will be on critical reading—leading to critical thinking and modeling strategies in school that mirror what historians do as they grapple with text—or if the richness of history will culminate in high-stakes tests that require memorization of large amounts of text.

Science

In science texts, as with other content texts, the reader must possess background knowledge of the subject and strategies for comprehension. As with all content courses, understanding science texts requires the reader to create mental representations. In science, comprehending causal relationships is particularly important to the reader's ability to make these mental representations. Specifically, understanding causal relationships as presented in science texts allows the student to order the information the text presents clearly and logically (León & Escudero, 2015). Understanding and visually representing all text patterns, specifically causal relationships, is essential.

Furthermore, science texts are replete with abstract concepts and mathematical language, making comprehension difficult for many students but further compounded for students with limited or incorrect science knowledge (León & Escudero, 2015). Therefore, before reading the text, students would benefit from investigating the concept through video clips, analogies, or clear explanations of critical ideas the teacher presented.

The ability to summarize critical information is essential in all content courses, but it has particular importance in science when precision is required in recalling and outlining information. Even more, the ability to summarize a text is a far better indication of the student's comprehension than their ability to respond to multiple-choice questions (León & Escudero, 2015). Therefore, teaching students to summarize crucial and secondary ideas in their science will go a long way toward enriching their mental representations of the text and showing their understanding of causal relationships.

The Peer-Assisted Learning Strategy (PALS) could be instrumental in helping students with text summarization (Vardy, Otaiba, Breadmore, Kung, Pétursdóttir, Zaru, & McMaster, 2022). There are multiple parts to this strategy. Here, I focus on only one of the elements called *shrink the paragraph*, a four-step process to summarize one sentence at a time and then present a summary of each paragraph. Recall the following sentence about mitosis from a previous example: "Mitosis is an important part of cell division that helps organisms grow and repair themselves" (Let's Talk Science, 2019). First, students underline the verb, which in this example is the word *is*. Second, they identify the who or what of the verb—that is, the person, place, or thing doing the action, which in the example is *mitosis*. Then, they identify two critical points of the who or what, which are *mitosis is an important part of cell division* and *mitosis helps organisms grow and repair themselves*. Students complete this process, one sentence at a time, and then summarize the two key points from the sentences in each paragraph. This is best learned in middle school to prepare students for more difficult texts once they enter high school.

As with the other disciplines, vocabulary poses a challenge for students in science texts. According to Kelly Grillo and Lisa Dieker (2013), to improve science literacy, teachers must explicitly teach vocabulary. Many science words are multisyllabic and involve parts that will likely need to be parsed in terms of the prefix and root word (Ortlieb & Cheek, 2013). Therefore, teaching students common science root words will benefit their comprehension of the science text. For example, students should be taught prefixes such as *anti*, meaning against; *dis*, meaning opposite; and *sub*, meaning under. They should also be taught roots such as *ology*, meaning the study of; *ject*, meaning to throw; and *graph*, meaning to record or write.

Conclusion

This chapter is a call to action for content-area teachers who have been well-trained on how to teach their content area, with perhaps less of a focus on comprehension skills unique to the discipline. Classroom teachers and literacy experts need to work together so that each one can support the other toward the goal of ensuring that students amass the skills needed to understand the content in the core discipline areas such as mathematics, social studies, and science. Whereas many generic strategies are effective across disciplines, it's equally important to learn the unique strategies of each discipline.

The next chapter explores strategic teaching, a thoughtful, slow-paced, and step-by step process whereby teachers recognize that for students to master skills, they need to learn the mental process or steps involved in the strategy.

Reading Instruction Across Content Areas: Next Steps

Strategy	How I will implement the strategy	Reflections
Generic strategies		
The PAR strategy		
Text structures		
Frontloading vocabulary		
Guiding questions		
Active reading		
Visualizing		

The Power of Effective Reading Instruction © 2024 Solution Tree Press • SolutionTree.com
Visit **go.SolutionTree.com/literacy** to download this free reproducible.

Strategy	How I will implement the strategy	Reflections
Making predictions		
Making connections		
Multimodal presentation of text		
Discipline-specific strategies		
MATHEMATICS		
Mathematics representation skills		
Math terms		
Math steps using I do, We do, You do one, You do many		

Strategy	How I will implement the strategy	Reflections
SOCIAL STUDIES		
SCIM-C		
Frayer diagram		
SCIENCE		
PALS		
Root words, prefixes, suffixes		

CHAPTER 6

STRATEGIC TEACHING AND LEARNING

I teach a graduate course in reading at McGill University in Montreal. In the course, I explore why students struggle to read, how to support them both inside and outside the classroom, the big 5 of reading, how to teach each of the big 5 reading strategies, and how to become a strategically minded reading teacher.

Each year, at the end of the semester, we identify the topics covered in class that will impact their teaching the most. They typically speak about more than one topic, often beginning with the importance of demystifying reading with the big 5. They express wishing they had known how to teach reading years ago but are happy to have resources to help all students, especially those who struggle. However, what rises to the top each year as the most important topic is strategic teaching; they speak about how this topic will change their teaching, not only regarding reading but in relation to all subjects.

Teaching strategically means providing the how-to or the steps involved in mastering a skill. Eventually, with effective how-to instruction, students will be able to apply the learning themselves, thus developing mastery of the skill. Teaching strategically is like giving students a gift. Students can take what they have learned and apply it so the learning continues. However, this is only successful if students can use the strategies independently of their teachers. The only way to ensure strategies become a gift to the student is if teachers guide students methodically and in a step-by-step way with the use of gradual release of responsibility.

Unfortunately, it is all too common for teachers to teach students new skills by talking for far too long—then, when the explanation is complete, presenting students with a few problems to work on independently. Students then start asking questions, one at a time, with many showing confusion right from the start.

As Lev Vygotsky (1978) explains in his influential social cognition theory, students become sophisticated comprehenders by observing experts using guided practice to perform complicated tasks (as cited in Concannon-Gibney & McCarthy, 2012). Strategic teaching, then, begins with naming the strategy you will present to students and then scaffolding the process in the form of steps until the student owns the strategy and can apply it autonomously. If we expect students to master reading, we need to teach strategically. Teachers need to overtly share with students their thinking as they model the steps required to master each strategy and explain to students why the strategy will be beneficial.

In this chapter, the focus is on metacognitive thinking—or thinking about thinking—while making sense of a text. The application of specific strategies, such as graphic organizers, are important and essential, but students need to be able to analyze each strategy for its utility given the task at hand (such as reading fiction versus expository text, reading for pleasure versus reading for an evaluation). The goal is for students to think about the strategies they are learning as essential tools and not just as worksheets to be completed. To that end, we examine the elements of strategic teaching, focusing on the steps to scaffold each strategy and transfer the expertise from teacher to student, ever so gradually. The focus is on what it means to be a strategically minded teacher, explicitly teaching the steps to strategic learning and how to use strategic instruction when presenting strategies.

Three Core Concepts

To set the stage for strategic teaching and learning, it's important to understand three core concepts: (1) the meaning of strategic teaching, (2) the critical characteristics of a strategic teacher, and (3) the essential elements of a strategic learner. In the second part of the chapter, I will describe the gradual release of responsibility model (I do, we do, you do one, you do many), which is one method used to teach strategically. (This model was touched on briefly in previous chapters.)

Strategic Teaching

Strategic teaching is a thoughtful, step-by-step process in which teachers recognize that for students to master skills, they need to learn the mental process or steps involved in the strategy, such as: read the text, summarize key elements, ask a question, clarify any difficult parts of the text, and then predict what the next passage with be about. Teachers guide students methodically and explicitly, beginning by naming the strategy and then explicitly teaching students each step involved in the process.

Research on the effectiveness of strategic, explicit instruction emerged in the 1980s due to an extensive review of the research leading to what was hoped to be a reconceptualization of reading instruction (Pearson & Dole, 1987). A review of the research on explicit comprehension instruction addressed the challenge of traditional methods of comprehension deemed ineffective because it focused on what these authors term *mentioning*, followed by practice, and then assessment (Pearson & Dole, 1987). A more progressive model of comprehension this review identified involves three essential elements, namely (1) direct explanation, (2) guided practice, and (3) transfer of what is learned to novel texts. Strategic, explicit teaching has been researched as a highly effective model for improving students' reading skills, and this model is effective for all elements of the big 5 of literacy. Students can and should be explicitly taught how language is divided into parts—starting with a sentence segmented into words, then words into syllables, and eventually individual sounds. Sound–letter correspondence, termed *phonics*, also needs to be explicitly taught, as do vocabulary, fluency, and comprehension. As an example, when students are explicitly taught Latin prefixes and suffixes, there is a noticeable improvement in their understanding (Castles et al., 2018). Finally, comprehension mastery depends on the explicit teaching of strategies with the gradual release of responsibility from teacher to student. More recently, research has posited that explicit teaching of strategies is more effective than self-discovery (Castles et al., 2018) and limited time is required, if taught effectively, for students to be able to apply the strategy.

However, despite this review of research dating back to the 1980s and many research studies since then on the effectiveness of strategic and explicit teaching, the traditional method of teaching reading strategies, particularly comprehension, remains centered around mentioning the strategy followed by practice and evaluation.

To become a strategic teacher, understanding the difference between a strategy and a skill is essential because strategic teachers teach strategies and not skills. With the effective teaching of literacy-based strategies, students should be able to master literacy skills such as phonemic awareness, phonics, vocabulary, fluency, and comprehension—but if not taught effectively, the majority of students will not (Moats, 2020).

Janice Almasi and Susan King Fullerton (2012), in their book *Teaching Strategic Processes in Reading*, cite the definition of *cognitive strategies* as "actions an individual selects deliberatively to attain a particular goal" (p. 1). Dole and colleagues (2009) define a cognitive strategy as "a mental routine or procedure for accomplishing a cognitive goal" (as cited in Almasi & Fullerton, 2012, p. 1). Dole's definition adds a critical element to the notion of strategic teaching, which is the set of routines or procedures needed to accomplish a task (Almasi & Fullerton, 2012).

In contrast, the term *skill* refers to "the ability to do something well," an aptitude that has been mastered (Skill, n.d.). According to Castles and colleagues (2018), the difference between a skill and strategy is essential to teachers' instructional practice. Skills are aptitudes that need to be acquired and can continue to be developed. For example, someone can master driving, but drivers can fit along a continuum from novice to expert. In other words, once learned, the skill can continue to be developed. However, strategies can be thought of as tricks that, once explained and modeled, can be accessible for use in multiple situations (Castles et al., 2018). Therefore, teaching a strategy using a modeled approach, including why the strategy is useful, helps students apply the strategy independently. Therefore, teachers do not teach students skills; instead, they teach strategies, which is the critical component, the essential ingredient that will lead students to master skills.

There are a few other vital differences between skills and strategies. Whereas strategies are slow, deliberate, metacognitive, effortful, and intentional actions, skills are fluid, automatic, and uninterrupted (Almasi & Fullerton, 2012). For example, beginning readers are effortfully working on decoding the words on the page or intentionally needing to employ strategies to comprehend what they're reading. Advanced readers, on the other hand, can read fluently and understand what they're reading with little effort. However, Almasi and Fullerton (2012) note that experienced readers may become slow and deliberate when tackling complex texts.

Additionally, perhaps most importantly, activities are not synonymous with strategies. Often, teachers are under the mistaken belief that an activity such as completing pages in a workbook will lead to mastery of a skill. What is essential in strategic work is students' knowledge of the strategy and when and how they should use it. The metacognitive nature of strategic teaching and learning is essential. Deliberate teaching of each strategy is necessary so students can later decide when to use each strategy toward mastery of the skill. This process is initially slow and intentional, but with a lot of practice, it will eventually become fluid and automatic. In this case, effective use of the strategy requires selecting, implementing, and monitoring its effectiveness.

Characteristics of a Strategic Teacher

Strategic teachers are master teachers—they have learned the art of strategic teaching. They realize that strategies must be named (for example, "I am going to teach you a new strategy called *text structure identification* that is helpful when trying to comprehend fact-based text"), and substantial time must be spent modeling the strategy so that students will eventually be able to apply it independent of the teacher. Also, master teachers are highly explicit in their teaching, leaving nothing to chance and making sure that they clearly, overtly, and sequentially state each step in the process.

At first, master teachers are deliberate and direct in their teaching, controlling most elements of the learning situation so that students can begin to apply the strategy without cognitive overload or too many expectations being placed on them too soon in the learning process. For example, if the student is learning a strategy for decod ing a text, and all of their efforts are on the strategies being taught to decode simple words (such as pointing to each letter and gradually blending the letters to form a word), the teacher would avoid asking the student a comprehension question. When we require students to apply too many strategies at once or when we call on them to examine too many features of text simultaneously, we overload their working memory. Avoiding this overload is essential for all students, specifically those struggling with working memory (Smith, Sáez, & Doabler, 2016).

Master teachers also recognize that deliberately teaching each strategy is necessary because if not, what is intended to be the instruction of a new strategy is actually giving students a command to do something. For example, an effective strategy for comprehending a text, and one of the elements of reciprocal teaching, is for the reader to ask themselves a question about a portion of the text they just read. Suppose a teacher instructs students to ask a question after reading a text without naming this as a strategy, showing students how to apply it, providing them with opportunities to apply it, and reinforcing its use. Students will likely see it as an order or something they've been told to do, and most students will attempt to do it to the best of their ability, but it won't be added to their toolbox of strategies for later use. On the other hand, with strategic teaching, students receive an explanation about why the strategy is beneficial. For example, the teacher might explain that under specific situations, a strategy should be applied (such as with fiction versus expository text) and the neces- sary steps (for example, "First you need to read the text, then you need to summarize the key ideas, and then you can ask yourself a question about what you just read to assess your understanding").

Another essential element of strategic teaching is the teacher's ability to select specific tasks that enable the instruction to move gradually from simple to more complex. This notion of gradual release of responsibility from the teacher to the student and not before the student has developed mastery of the target strategy is of paramount importance to the learner and has been extrapolated from the field of psychology. A specific model that uses this gradual release of responsibility is explained in the next section of this chapter.

According to theorists such as Ivan Pavlov (1927), B. F. Skinner (1938), and Albert Bandura (1977), each one with their own unique theories but collectively examining the acquisition of learning, strategic teaching that focuses on explicitly stating what students will learn and how they will learn it leaves the learner feeling competent and with a positive feeling about the learning.

The authors Céline Guilmois, Maria Popa-Roch, Céline Clément, Steve Bissonnette, and Bertrand Troadec (2019) examine the benefits of strategic teaching using a mathematics example. When students are taught multiplication tables, which is initially a neutral stimulus for students who have not had previous experience with it, their response may be one of stress or feelings of inadequacy. Their negative feelings may be linked not only to the content of multiplication tables but also to the condition under which the learning took place, leaving the student with a negative feeling toward mathematics. Learning is highly connected to emotional state, and thus students' belief about themselves is highly connected to their success as students (Guilmois, Popa-Roch, Clément, Bissonnette, & Troadec, 2019).

Additionally, strategic teachers support students by using effective guidance rather than being overly directive in their interactions with students. Let's use the reciprocal teaching example of questioning again. Suppose a student just read a text about a horse race with a horse named Lucky, who won his fifth race in a row. As written in the text, Lucky is now getting older and would probably not be able to compete in many more races. When prompted to ask a question about the passage, a student with poor comprehension might ask, "What time of year did this race take place?" rather than say, "It doesn't say that in the text—you need to ask a question like, Why is the horse probably not going to continue competing in races in the future?"

A master teacher would likely request that the student asking this question reread the passage while asking the student a question, for example: "Is the answer to your question in the text?" If the student replies that the answer to the question isn't there, the teacher would then follow with another guided question, not specific to this text: "What important facts did you just read in the text?" Remember that the answers students give to your questions will probably serve as your summary of the essential parts of the passage. These questions are more effective because they can guide the student when reading other texts and are not specific to this particular text.

When I present workshops on reciprocal teaching, teachers often question the benefit of this type of specific questioning and prefer that students infer meaning after reading a portion of text. However, the skill of questioning related to information found in the text is essential because students need to focus on details of the text prior to going deeper and being able to make inferences about the text.

Finally, master teachers know they need to teach students how to implement the strategy. Referring back to the earlier definition of strategy as a "mental routine or procedure," students need to learn the steps of the procedure. Therefore, an accurate depiction of a master teacher is someone who consistently instructs students on how to master the steps of diverse strategies. In this sense, master teachers are how-to educators, teaching students reading strategies such as decoding simple CVC words, reading fluently, making predictions, formulating questions about the text, and understanding how to make personal connections.

Many years ago, in one of my graduate classes, a student challenged me that not all strategies have steps that can be followed. She noted that backward problem solving didn't include specific steps. I asked her to write out an example of backward problem solving—and solve it—but I asked her to say each step out loud as she did. Without realizing it, she responded with, "First, I have to . . ."

The Strategic Learner

Extensive research exists on the importance of teaching students to become strategic learners, able to learn a range of strategies from phonemic segmentation to text comprehension (Anwar, 2020; Martin-Kniep & Picone-Zocchia, 2009). To become proficient readers, students need to master the knowledge of printed words, including phonemic awareness as the foundation. They also need to learn the connection between letters and sounds and how sounds map onto letters or graphemes to form words and learn to read fluently and without too many errors so they'll have sufficient resources to focus on comprehension. Reading comprehension requires knowledge of many strategies and the metacognitive ability to identify when each should be applied. Equally critical, monitoring comprehension is essential to ascertain if there has been a breakdown in understanding.

Strategic readers possess essential characteristics learned over time, which eventually become an inherent part of their repertoire (Almasi & Fullerton, 2012). These characteristics include the following.

- Strategic learners know many different reading strategies and are motivated to apply them. Essential to motivation, specifically regarding reading, is interest in the material and a history of success using diverse strategies.

- To remain motivated, tasks assigned to strategic learners must be at the right level of challenge. If the task is too easy, the student will become bored, but if it's too challenging, the student may become overly anxious and give up.

- The goal must be clear, and strategic learners should be rewarded with praise for their efforts.

- Strategic learners are aware of what it means to be metacognitive and how to apply metacognition to monitor their use of strategies. These learners can apply the correct strategy according to the reading task. For example, they know specific strategies for text types, such as expository or narrative texts.

- Strategic learners possess grit and perseverance. They have a goal in mind and can overcome challenges in pursuing their goals, such as understanding complex text.

The ultimate goal of strategic teaching is for students to become strategic learners who learn one strategy, at a time, to mastery. Eventually, students will amass many strategies, enabling them to become adept at deciding when to use which one. Without this latter part of being able to decide which strategy to use when, students will gather a plethora of strategies but not have the metacognitive decision-making ability to decide when to apply the different strategies (Almasi & Fullerton, 2012).

Gradual Release of Responsibility

Remember that one aspect of being a strategic teacher is telling students explicitly what they will learn and showing them how they will do it. For reading strategies, this always includes specific steps or procedures that students need to master. An excellent process for accomplishing this is the gradual release of responsibility (Pearson & Gallagher, 1983) from teacher to student called *I do, we do, you do one, you do many,* which has been mentioned in earlier chapters, that enables teachers to teach strategically so that students can become strategic learners (Fisher & Frey, 2021). The next section goes into more detail about this process.

When teaching explicitly, teachers control the learning conditions. In the gradual release of responsibility model, the teacher initially takes full responsibility for the learning as they engage in a think-aloud with students. Then, students participate in guided practice with simple examples before the teacher presents more complex ones. Students are gradually given responsibility for the task in a slow and deliberate fashion, ensuring that they are able to accomplish it with relative success. The model therefore requires proficiency in the art of scaffolding. As student competence increases, so does the complexity of the task, and as a result, the learning situation produces positive feelings toward the learning. Equally important is the ongoing feedback that the learner receives throughout this process. As the student moves through the learning sequence, they receive constant feedback, eventually leading to correct practice and automaticity. The development of automaticity is essential because the learner can then offload simpler tasks, leaving mental energy and resources for more complete ones (Guilmois et al., 2019).

According to Torgesen (2004), this explicit teaching model is "instruction that does not leave anything to chance and does not make assumptions about skills and knowledge that students will acquire on their own" (p. 363). Additionally, the teacher presents material overtly, so students are clearly informed that they are going to learn the steps required to master a skill. Then, steps are clearly presented to students: I do, we do, you do one, you do many. This method has been subject to a lot of research, and results indicate that it is a powerful method to teach students to read (Reutzel, Child, Jones, & Clark, 2014). Furthermore, it is based on two earlier models of instruction, direct teaching and direct explanation.

Direct teaching incorporates seven steps into the process: (1) a step-by-step explanation of strategies, (2) an opportunity for students to master each step in the process, (3) corrective feedback based on student errors, (4) scaffolded support that involves gradual fading of teacher activities, (5) practice with many different types of examples, (6) review of student mastery, and (7) pre-correction of potential student errors (Stockard et al., 2018).

A direct explanation is the teacher's explanation of the process when implementing a particular strategy. The elements of these two approaches are essential to the successful implementation of this model. A meta-analysis that includes eleven meta-analyses (thus hundreds of research studies) of the most effective approaches in supporting students who are at risk in the areas of reading, writing, and mathematics indicates that this explicit teaching model and reciprocal teaching are the most effective pedagogical approaches (Bissonnette, Richard, Gauthier, & Bouchard, 2010).

This approach can be divided into three stages: (1) modeled examples, (2) directed practice, and (3) autonomous practice (Bissonnette et al., 2010). Modeled examples occur during the *I do* phase, directed practice occurs during *we do* and *you do one* phases, and autonomous practice occurs during the *you do many* phase. The following sections present it in more detail.

I Do

The *I do* step begins with the teacher ensuring that they have their students' attention. Laptops are closed, pens are placed on the desk, and all other distractions are removed. During this phase, teachers tell students what they need to know about the strategy and how to apply it. This step is short but critical because explicit instruction involves demonstrating the steps of the strategy and modeling one's own thinking. Said brilliantly by Joseph Hart, "We have plenty of people who teach what they know, but very few who can teach their own capacity to learn" (Joseph Hart as cited in Littky, 2004). Students are expected to listen carefully to the think-aloud as the teacher completes it.

If a student appears to be advanced in a particular area, they can "test out." This means they would be evaluated on the skill to see if they have already learned it. Additionally, teachers can use universal screening to assess mastery of the skill. If mastered, students receive challenging material to complete that requires applying this skill while others develop proficiency. For example, suppose the teacher is teaching the steps of a comprehension strategy such as reciprocal teaching or PALS (explained in chapters 4 and 5, pages 81 and 97), and a group of students have shown mastery of the strategy. In that case, they could be asked to complete a writing assignment on a book they're reading.

In this first step, the teacher takes full responsibility for the learning, asking herself questions and answering them. For example, the teacher might ask herself out loud, "How do I know if this is a good question to ask myself to check my understanding?" The teacher would then answer, "I'll need to see if the answer is in the text. Also, if the answer to the question is a small detail that is insignificant to the meaning of the text, I should probably find another question." For the entire dialogue, see table 6.1 (page 134). Finally, visual displays are helpful at this stage. For example, when teaching PALS, the teacher should display the four steps of the process on the board.

We Do

As mentioned, this model requires the gradual release of responsibility for the task from the teacher to the student. Therefore, once the teacher has modeled the steps with her think-aloud, it is time for the students to complete a different example, applying the same steps as a group and with the teacher facilitating. For example, the teacher will have another sentence on the board along with the steps to shrink the paragraph using PALS. The teacher informs the students that no one needs to raise their hand and that all students should answer simultaneously. The teacher will pay attention to see if all students are speaking and make a mental note if any student is not. More or less in unison, students will work through each step, modeling the actions applied by the teacher. Students say the steps explicitly; for example, students should be heard stating, "First, I have to read the sentence and underline the verb—so *run* should be underlined. Second, I need to ask who or what is doing the action—and circle that word. Third, I need to find one or two essential facts about the who or the what." Essentially, they copy the teacher's process using a different example.

You Do One

This step is for students to show their ability to complete an example independently and correctly. For the same strategy of PALS shrink the paragraph, another sentence is written on the board. At this point, students are expected to read the sentence and underline, highlight, and square each part of a sentence according to the teacher's example. Students need to complete one example before moving on to the next because, as Vince Lombardi, the famous football coach, suggested, to perfect a skill, a lot of perfect practice is required (Lombardi, as cited in Kannings, 2014). Practicing a skill incorrectly will lead to the incorrect development of that skill. Before asking students to do many examples and hopefully develop automaticity, teachers must give students feedback on one example to ensure that they've completed it correctly. Often, this point is where teachers identify confusion or misunderstandings. Feedback is indispensable at this stage to prevent students from consolidating the strategy incorrectly.

You Do Many

At this point, students should know the steps to the strategy and be able to do at least one example correctly, without error. For instance, with our PALS shrink the paragraph example, students should have heard the teacher model one example, completed another example with classmates, completed one on their own, and are now ready to do many examples. This last step is essential to developing automaticity. At this point, the teacher provides students with multiple examples to complete. Again, with our PALS shrink the paragraph example, the teacher gives students a paragraph, and students then apply the strategy to each sentence.

Throughout the process, it's imperative to remind students how to apply the strategy and when it's most effective. For example, a strategy may be most effective under certain conditions. Once students have mastered the strategy, teachers should present varied texts and prompt students to apply the various strategies they've learned as appropriate to the text.

Table 6.1 shows the complete process of gradual release of responsibility using the PALS shrink the paragraph example. This example could be used in middle school as well. When teaching a new strategy, always use a simple text. Table 6.2 (page 136) shows an example of this model for literacy support in high school.

TABLE 6.1: Gradual Release of Responsibility Explicit Teaching Steps and Dialogue—Elementary Example

STEPS	SAMPLE TEACHER SCRIPT AND STUDENT RESPONSE	WRITTEN ON THE BOARD WITH COMPLETED STUDENT WORK
I do	Teacher: Please close your laptops and notebooks and put your pencils on your desk. Nothing should be in your hands. All of your attention should be focused on me. We will learn the PALS shrink the paragraph, a beneficial strategy for reading comprehension. The steps are written on the board. Teacher: The benefit of the strategy is to help you identify the subject of each sentence and a few essential details about the subject. The subject is not always easy to find in a sentence. Sometimes it's at the beginning of the sentence, such as *Johnny ate an apple*, but sometimes the subject could be hard to find, such as, *After the flood, I bought new furniture.* Teacher: As you see on the board, the sentence is *Johnny is running home*. First, I read the sentence: *Johnny is running home*. Then, I underline the action or verb of the sentence. In this sentence, the action is running, so I will underline the word *running*. Third, I ask myself, "Who is running?" Johnny is running, so I am going to circle the word *Johnny*. If I see *is running* or *will run*, I will underline the two words because, as we learned, they're both parts of the verb [the teacher is identifying possible difficulties]. Fourth, I need to put a square around one or two essential things about Johnny. I will put a square around *running home*.	Shrink the paragraph strategy: 1. Underline the verb. 2. Circle the who or the what (who or what is doing the action). 3. Put a square around the one or two most important things about the who or the what. 4. Summarize the paragraph in ten words or less using the ideas in step 3.

We do	Teacher: Now we're going to complete an example together. I am going to write a sentence on the board, and I'm going to ask everyone to list the steps. You don't need to raise your hand. I'll say, "The first step is . . ." and I want you all to tell me what the first step is. Remember to say it at the same time. [The teacher writes *Fran is eating an apple* on the board.] Teacher: The first step is . . . Students: Read the sentence. [All students read the sentence out loud. The teacher looks around to see if any student is not speaking.] Teacher: The second step is . . . Students: Find the verb . . . *is eating.* Teacher: That's excellent; you remembered to include the complete verb *is eating*. The third step is . . . Students: Who is eating? . . . *Fran.* You need to put a circle around *Fran.* Teacher: What are important things about Fran? She is eating an apple. So you need to put a square around *eating an apple.*	(Fran) is [eating] an apple.
You do one	On the board, the teacher writes, *Last year, Elena ran the Boston Marathon with her friend*. The students look at the steps written on the board and follow the steps. The teacher walks around and provides feedback to students as needed.	Last year, (Elena) ran [the Boston Marathon] with her friend.
You do many	Teacher: I copied the steps for each of you. Make sure to put the sheet of steps in your binder. On the second sheet, you'll see a paragraph. Follow the steps we've just done for each sentence in the paragraph. Once you've completed the steps for each sentence, write a summary of the sentence with all the points you've squared. Make sure that your summary is no more than ten words.	Yesterday, Simon ran to the store to buy apples for his apple cake recipe. The apples were bruised, but he bought them anyway. He was sure that bruised apples were just fine when baking a cake. He got home and told his mother that the apples were bruised, and she confirmed that bruised apples are fine when baking a cake.

TABLE 6.2: Gradual Release of Responsibility Explicit Teaching Steps and Dialogue—
High School Example

STEPS	SAMPLE TEACHER SCRIPT AND STUDENT RESPONSE	WRITTEN ON THE BOARD WITH COMPLETED STUDENT WORK
I do	Teacher: Please close your laptops and notebooks and put your pens on your desk. Nothing should be in your hands. All of your attention should be focused on me. We will learn the SCIM-C strategy, which stands for Summarize, Contextualize, Infer, Monitor, and Corroborate. The steps are written on the board. Teacher: The benefit of the strategy is to provide you with a method to understand historical documents. During each stage of this process, you will focus on a diverse aspect of the document such that at the end of the four-step process, you will be better able to understand essential elements of the document, the intended audience, when it was written, and the reliability of the source. Teacher: Let's look at the document (Treaty of Versailles). I'm going to model the four steps involved in the SCIM-C strategy. As you can see on the board and on your guide sheet, **the first step** in the process is summarizing. I am going to skim the document and ask myself these questions: What type of document is this? Is it primary meaning an original document or is it secondary meaning a summary of the original document? I can see from the wording, year written, and language used that it is a primary document. What perspective is provided? Upon reading the first few sentences, and looking at the signors of the document, I can see that it is written from the perspective of the four leaders. Why was this document written? If I look at part one in the document, I can see that it was written to enhance the cooperation, peace among the nations, and a sense of security following the devastation of World War I. Who wrote the document? The allied powers wrote the document. **The second step** in the SCIM-C strategy is contextualizing. Since we are using a primary document, that may not include the context, you may need to conduct a search to learn about the context of the treaty. In our session last week with the librarian, she taught us how to find reliable sources. Take out your information sheet to help you here. I can see from the primary document that the treaty was signed on June 28, 1919. If I do a little bit of a search, I see that the United States signed another peace treaty with Germany because there were objections to the Treaty of Versailles that were not addressed. The next question under contextualizing is, What historical question is	SCIM-C strategy: 1. Summarize 2. Contextualize 3. Infer 4. Monitor 5. Corroborate The specific questions to ask for each section are listed on the board. Students also have their own paper copies of each step.

STEPS	SAMPLE TEACHER SCRIPT AND STUDENT RESPONSE	WRITTEN ON THE BOARD WITH COMPLETED STUDENT WORK
	intended to be answered? How did the major nations attempt to end the war and create a world with greater cooperation, security, and peace? The last question to answer here is, What was happening historically during the time the document was written? Again, if I do a small search, I can see that the document was written to end the war that devastated many countries and caused significant death. The war was initiated between Serbia and Austro-Hungary after the assassination of an Austro-Hungarian leader. Other countries entered the war and it led to a conflict between the Central Powers and the Allies. **The third step** in the process is Inferring: What points of view are presented in the document? I looked through the document, but what I really want to see is who signed it. I can see that it was signed by the Allies but also by Germany. But again, if I do a little search, I see that the United States didn't sign the treaty. I've already looked this up so I'm just confirming it here. I also read that Germany did not participate in the writing of the treaty but was pressured to sign or risk entering back into war. The next question in this section asks, Was anything omitted that should have been included in the document? It is a long document so it's difficult for me to identify if anything isn't there. However, based on what I read in the document and what I learned from my additional searches, I would like to see clearly in the document that it wasn't signed by the United States and that Germany didn't have a permanent role in the writing of the treaty. **The fourth step** in the process is monitoring. Now, I need to use my metacognitive skills. We spoke about this and discussed the importance of thinking about what you know and understand about what you've learned. I feel like I know the brief details of how the war started and the basic details of the treaty. However, I would like to know more about how the Treaty of Versailles contributed to the start of World War II. **The fifth step** is corroborating. Here I ask myself if this document is similar to other documents that I've read or seen. In this class we've learned about other treaties such as the Treaty of Paris. There are definitely some similarities, most notably the reparations Germany needed to pay to the Allies. Finally, the last question is, What additional sources of information are needed to understand the context? As I mentioned previously, I would like to learn more about the relationship between the Treaty of Versailles and the start of World War II.	

continued →

STEPS	SAMPLE TEACHER SCRIPT AND STUDENT RESPONSE	WRITTEN ON THE BOARD WITH COMPLETED STUDENT WORK
We do	Teacher: Now, we're going to complete an example together. I will show you a short passage from another document, and we'll review the steps together. Remember that you don't need to raise your hand. I want to hear all of you at the same time. Make sure to include the steps such as, the first part of the strategy is to summarize. Here are the questions we need to ask ourselves: After we ask each question, we'll look for the information in the text. We will look at the Transcript of the Wannsee Conference on January 20, 1942. Teacher: Let's go. You would start with . . . Students: The first thing we need to do is to skim the document and look for images if they are there. Read the headings, dates, names, and any other information. Teacher: Excellent, continue! Students: The first step is to summarize. We have to ask ourselves, What type of document is it? It is a transcript from the original conference. I can see from the document that it was top secret. The second question is, What perspective is provided in the document? From the names of the people at the conference, I assume it was the perspective of the top officials of the Nazi party. Students continue going through each step in the process with the teacher's encouragement. The teacher would likely need to remind students of missing steps. The teacher would also pay attention to any student who is not participating.	SCIM-C steps and questions (handout) Historical document
You do one	The teacher tells the students that she wants them to practice the SCIM-C strategy independently. She reminds them to follow each of the steps and ask and respond in writing to each question. She then gives them another document. This time, students will use an editorial from a British newspaper about the Munich Agreement between Hitler and Chamberlain in 1938. Again, students will be instructed to follow the steps in SCIM-C.	SCIM-C sheet with questions (handout) Historical document Editorial
You do many	This time, the teacher will provide students with shorter documents, preferably a few paragraphs, and ask them to practice these skills independently. The teacher will again remind students of each step and the questions they need to ask themselves and document in writing. Once completed, the teacher could ask students to work in pairs and discuss their responses.	SCIM-C strategy and questions (handout) Short documents

Conclusion

The evidence is clear. Research has found that explicit teaching of foundational skills in reading, namely the big 5, benefits all students, especially those at risk for gaps in reading skills. Given the effectiveness of this approach in enabling students to become strategic learners, teachers would be far better off applying this explicit teaching instructional approach when teaching the big 5 of reading. Strategic teaching should begin with foundational skills but shouldn't end there. Strategic teaching of language skills such as vocabulary and specific comprehension strategies (many of these are mentioned in chapter 4, page 81) must become a focus in high school content classes (Concannon-Gibney & McCarthy, 2012).

Just as we expect teachers to move away from the mention, practice, and assessment cycle where the strategy is stated, students engage in limited practice, and then they are assessed for their mastery of the skill and often not even the strategy itself, so must our teacher education programs move away from this cycle. If teachers are to successfully instruct students on how to master the essential elements of reading, they must be taught in teacher education programs how to do so. Decades of research have crystallized around the need to explicitly teach students the strategies they need to master early literacy development. This will leave them with the resources to tackle more sophisticated reading development skills. University classrooms teaching future teachers to tackle the critical task of teaching students to read—a task that is by many accounts the most vital skill students will be expected to learn in school—need to reflect the consensus that the research has solidified. We need to teach future teachers how to become strategic educators, explicitly teaching students to become sophisticated, strategic readers equipped with an abundance of evidence-based strategies to stand them in good stead to become readers who love reading.

Strategic Teaching and Learning: Next Steps

Strategic teaching phase	How I will implement this model (identify a specific example)	Reflections
I do		
We do		
You do one		
You do many		

EPILOGUE

In November 2022, after I presented a session on reading at a conference, a woman approached me to tell me that she was using many of the evidence-based approaches I presented at my session; however, she seemed unsure about whether or not she was doing the right thing because her sister, also a teacher, was using the sight-word approach, convinced this was the best way to teach reading. I have had similar conversations with people across the globe who believe that the jury is still out on the best approach to teaching reading. Nothing could be further from the truth, as this book has shown: the neuroscience of teaching provides us with necessary clarity.

Teaching students to read is the most essential duty of schools, yet over 20 percent of students struggle to read, with additional students at risk for developing reading problems (Moats, 2020). The tragedy of reading failure is that it is preventable (Dehaene et al., 2015; Moats, 2020; Shaywitz & Shaywitz, 2020; Urquhart & Frazee, 2012; Witter, 2013). Thanks to extensive research conducted since the early 1980s, great consensus exists on how students learn to read, instructional methods that teachers should apply in the classroom, evidence-based reading materials they should use, and models such as RTI that schools and teachers can implement to ensure that instruction and remediation incorporate the best elements of literacy-based teaching.

Equally important, reading is not only the literacy teacher's responsibility but everyone's business. Reading instruction begins in the early years when students must learn fundamental elements of basic reading. Most grade 1 students will be able to comprehend grade-level texts if they are proficient in accurate word reading. However, as students move through the grades, both general and discipline-specific skills are essential such as background knowledge, vocabulary, and metacognitive thinking (Moats, 2020). Therefore, students need to be immersed in the world of literacy, exposed to diverse fiction and non-fiction texts, and taught how to employ effective strategies.

There needs to be a path forward to escape the current grim literacy statistics. The design of pre-service and in-service teacher programs should be informed by research and focus on the essential elements of reading and evidence-based instructional practices and materials. Reading courses in teacher preparation programs should not be limited to language teachers; rather, they should be mandatory for all teachers.

Teachers need to be empowered to assess student reading levels to ascertain if they're reaching grade-level benchmarks across the reading trajectory. By combining this knowledge with knowledge of why some students struggle to read and remediation programs to support them, we can significantly lower the reading failure rate in our schools.

As a final note, and said so powerfully by Moats (2020), "Teaching reading is rocket science. But it is also established science with clear, specific, practical instructional strategies that all teachers should be taught and supported in using." Reading failure can be prevented; we know better, and therefore we must do better.

REFERENCES AND RESOURCES

Abu-Rabia, S., & Siegel, L. S. (2002). Reading, syntactic, orthographic, and working memory skills of bilingual Arabic-English speaking Canadian children. *Journal of Psycholinguistic Research, 31*(6), 661–678. https://doi.org/10.1023/A:1021221206119

Adams, M. J. (1990). Beginning to read: Thinking and learning. *Psychological Review, 65,* 197–208.

Adler, M. J. (1940). *How to read a book: the art of getting a liberal education.* New York: Simon and Schuster.

Agarwal, S., Sair, H. I., Gujar, S., & Pillai, J. J. (2019). Language mapping with fMRI: Current standards and reproducibility. *Topics in Magnetic Resonance Imaging, 28*(4), 225–233. https://doi.org/10.1097/RMR.0000000000000216

Al Otaiba, S., Kosanovich, M. L., Torgesen, J. K., Kamhi, A. G., & Catts, H. W. (2012). Assessment and instruction for phonemic awareness and word recognition skills. *Language and Reading Disabilities, 3,* 112–140.

Allington, R. L., McCuiston, K., & Billen, M. (2015). What research says about text complexity and learning to read. *The Reading Teacher, 68*(7), 491–501. https://doi .org/10.1002/trtr.1280

Almasi, J. F., & King Fullerton, S. (2012). *Teaching strategic processes in reading* (2nd ed.). New York: The Guilford Press.

Al-Shidhani, T. A., & Arora, V. (2012). Understanding dyslexia in children through human development theories. *Sultan Qaboos University Medical Journal, 12*(3), 286–294. Accessed at https://www.ncbi.nlm.nih.gov/pmc/articles/PMC3529662/ on April 5, 2023.

American Psychiatric Association. (2013). *Diagnostic and statistical manual of mental disorders* (5th ed.). Washington, DC: Author.

Annie E. Casey Foundation. (2010). *EARLY WARNING! Why reading by the end of third grade matters.* Baltimore: Author. Accessed at www.aecf.org/resources/early-warning -why-reading-by-the-end-of-third-grade-matters on October 4, 2023.

Anwar, A. K. (2020). The effect of collaborative strategic reading toward students [*sic*] reading skill. *Anglophile Journal, 1*(1), 21–28. https://journal.uniku.ac.id/index.php /ERJEE/article/view/7549/3572

Archer, A. L., & Hughes, C. A. (2011). *Explicit instruction: Effective and efficient teaching.* New York: The Guilford Press.

Armstrong, A. (2015). Forward. In V. Bozsik (Ed.), *Improving literacy skills across learning.* CIDREE yearbook 2015. Budapest: Hungarian Institute for Educational Research and Development. Accessed at www.cidree.org/fileadmin/files/pdf/publications /YB_15_Improving_Literacy_Skills_Across_Learning.pdf on April 5, 2023.

Aslam, F. (2018). Difficulties of dyslexic students at secondary level in our education system. *International Bulletin of Linguistics and Literature (IBLL), 1*(4), 16–26.

Avalos, B., Bengochea, J., & Secada, W. G. (2015). *Bilingual education for social justice: A framework for policy and practice.* New York: Teachers College Press.

Avalos, B., Bengochea, J., & Secada, W. G. (2015). Theorizing the intersections of language, culture, and power in bilingual education. *Bilingual Research Journal, 38*(1), 3–22.

Avalos, M. A., Bengochea, A., & Secada, W. G. (2015). Reading mathematics: More than words and clauses; more than numbers and symbols on a page. In K. L. Santi & D. K. Reed (Eds.), *Improving reading comprehension of middle and high school students* (pp. 49–74). New York: Springer.

Bailey, A. L. (Ed.). (2007). *The language demands of school: Putting academic English to the test.* New Haven, CT: Yale University Press.

Balu, R., Zhu, P., Doolittle, F., Schiller, E., Jenkins, J., & Gersten, R. (2015). *Evaluation of response to intervention practices for elementary school reading* (NCEE 2016–4000). Washington, DC: National Center for Education Evaluation and Regional Assistance, Institute of Education Sciences, U.S. Department of Education. Accessed at https:// files.eric.ed.gov/fulltext/ED560820.pdf on April 5, 2023.

Bandura, A. (1977). *Social learning theory.* Englewood Cliffs, NJ: Prentice Hall.

Barrio, B. L., Lindo, E. J., Combes, B. H., & Hovey, K. A. (2015). Ten years of response to intervention: Implications for general education teacher preparation programs. *Action in Teacher Education, 37*(2), 190–204. https://doi.org/10.1080/01626620.201 5.1004603

Baumann, J. F., Edwards, E. C., Boland, E. M., Olejnik, S., & Kame'enui, E. J. (2003). Vocabulary tricks: Effects of instruction in morphology and context on fifth-grade students' ability to derive and infer word meanings. *American Educational Research Journal, 40*(2), 447–494. https://doi.org/10.3102/00028312040002447

Beers, K. (2003). *When kids can't read: What teachers can do.* Portsmouth, NH: Heinemann.

Ben-Shachar, M., Dougherty, R. F., Deutsch, G. K., & Wandell, B. A. (2011). The development of cortical sensitivity to visual word forms. *J Cogn Neurosci, 23*(9): 2387–2399. https://doi.org/10.1162/jocn.2011.21615

Benedict, A. E., Brownell, M., Bettini, E., & Sohn, H. (2021). Learning together: Teachers' evolving understanding of Coordinated Word Study Instruction within an RTI framework. *Teacher Education and Special Education, 44*(2), 134–159.

Biemiller, A., & Boote, C. (2006). An effective method for building meaning vocabulary in primary grades. *Journal of Educational Psychology, 98*(1), 44–62. https://doi.org /10.1037/0022-0663.98.1.44

Bissonnette, S., Richard, M., Gauthier, C., & Bouchard, C. (2010). Quelles sont les stratégies d'enseignement efficaces favorisant les apprentissages fondamentaux auprès des élèves en difficulté de niveau élémentaire ? Résultats d'une méga-analyse. *Revue de recherche appliquée sur l'apprentissage, 3*(1), 1–35. Accessed at https://www.treaq.ca /wp-content/uploads/2019/05/Article3_steeve_bissonn_2010.pdf on April 5, 2023.

Bogaerds-Hazenberg, S. T. M., Evers-Vermeul, J., & van den Bergh, H. (2021). A meta-analysis on the effects of text structure instruction on reading comprehension in the upper elementary grades. *Reading Research Quarterly, 56*(3), 435–462. https://doi .org/10.1002/rrq.311

Boonen, A. J. H., de Koning, B. B., Jolles, J., & van der Schoot, M. (2016). Word problem solving in contemporary math education: A plea for reading comprehension skills training. *Frontiers in Psychology, 7*, 191. https://doi.org/10.3389/fpsyg.2016 .00191

Boot, F. H., Owuor, J., Dinsmore, J., & MacLachlan, M. (2018). Access to assistive technology for people with intellectual disabilities: A systematic review to identify barriers and facilitators. *Journal of Intellectual Disability Research, 62*(10), 900–921. https://doi.org/10.1111/jir.12532

Bowers, J. S. (2020). Reconsidering the evidence that systematic phonics is more effective than alternative methods of reading instruction. *Educational Psychology Review, 32*(3), 681–705. https://doi.org/10.1007/s10648-019-09515-y

Brignoni-Perez, E., Jamal, N. I., & Eden, G. F. (2020). An fMRI study of English and Spanish word reading in bilingual adults. *Brain and Language, 202*, Article 104725. https://doi.org/10.1016/j.bandl.2019.104725

Bryson, B. (1990). *Mother tongue: English & how it got that way.* New York: William Morrow.

Buffum, A., Mattos, M., & Malone, J. (2012). *Simplifying response to intervention: Four essential guiding principles.* Bloomington, IN: Solution Tree Press.

Buffum, A., Mattos, M., & Malone, J. (2018). *Taking action: A handbook for RTI at work.* Bloomington, IN: Solution Tree Press.

Burt, C. (1937). *The backward child.* London: University of London Press.

Butler, K. (2022). A hypothesis of reading instruction as a cause of dyslexia. *Journal of Education and Learning, 11*(2), 54–62. https://doi.org/10.5539/jel.v11n2p54

Calderón, M. E., & Slakk, S. (2018). *Teaching reading to English learners, grades 6–12: A framework for improving achievement in the content areas.* Thousand Oaks, CA: Corwin.

Castles, A., Rastle, K., & Nation, K. (2018). Ending the reading wars: Reading acquisition from novice to expert. *Psychological Science in the Public Interest, 19*(1), 5–51. https://doi.org/10.1177/1529100618772271

Church, J. A., Coalson, R. S., Lugar, H. M., Petersen, S. E., & Schlaggar, B. L. (2008). A developmental fMRI study of reading and repetition reveals changes in phonological and visual mechanisms over age. *Cerebral Cortex, 18*(9), 2054–2065. https://doi.org/10.1093/cercor/bhm228

Church, J. A., Coalson, R. S., Lugar, H. M., Petersen, S. E., & Schlaggar, B. L. (2008). Functional MRI of the development of reading skills. *Journal of Cognitive Neuroscience, 20*(10), 1907–1922.

Chyl, K., Gentile, F., Dębska, A., Dynak, A., Łuniewska, M., Wójcik, M., et al. (2023). Early reading skills and the ventral occipito-temporal cortex organization. *Cortex, 160,* 134–151.

Clemens, N. H., Solari, E. J., Kearns, D. M., Fien, H., Nelson, N. J., Stalega, M. V., et al. (2021). They say you can do phonemic awareness instruction "in the dark," but should you? A critical evaluation of the trend toward advanced phonemic awareness training. PsyArXiv Preprints. Accessed at https://psyarxiv.com/ajxbv on June 26, 2023. https://doi.org/10.31234/osf.io/ajxbv

Cohen, J. (1988). *Statistical power analysis for the behavioral sciences* (2nd ed.). Hillside, NJ: Lawrence Erlbaum Associates.

Colorado Education Initiative. (n.d.). *Five expository text structures and their associated signal words.* Accessed at www.coloradoedinitiative.org/wp-content/uploads/2014/04/LDC-Text-Structure-Guide.pdf on May 25, 2023.

Colvin, R. L., & Helfand, D. (1999, December 12). Special education in state is failing on many fronts. *Los Angeles Times.* Accessed at https://www.latimes.com/archives/la-xpm-1999-dec-12-mn-43238-story.html on April 6, 2023.

Concannon-Gibney, T., & McCarthy, M. J. (2012). The explicit teaching of reading comprehension in science class: A pilot professional development program. *Improving Schools, 15*(1), 73–88. https://doi.org/10.1177/1365480211433726

Connor, C. M., Alberto, P. A., Compton, D. L., & O'Connor, R. E. (2014). *Improving reading outcomes for students with or at risk for reading disabilities: A synthesis of the contributions from the institute of education sciences research centers* (NCSER 2014–3000). Washington, DC: National Center for Special Education Research, Institute of Education Sciences, U.S. Department of Education. Accessed at https://files.eric.ed.gov/fulltext/ED544759.pdf on April 6, 2023.

Connors-Tadros, L. (2014, May). Definitions and approaches to measuring reading proficiency. Center on Enhancing Early Learning Outcomes. Accessed at http://ceelo .org/wp-content/uploads/2014/05/ceelo_fast_fact_reading_proficiency.pdf on April 6, 2023.

Cuttance, P. (1998). Quality assurance reviews as a catalyst for school improvement in Australia. In A. Hargreaves, A. Lieberman, M. Fullan, & D. Hopkins (Eds.), *International handbook of educational change* (Volume 5, pp. 1135–1162). New York: Springer.

Daroczy, G., Wolska, M., Meurers, W. D., & Nuerk, H. (2015). Word problems: A review of linguistic and numerical factors contributing to their difficulty. *Frontiers in Psychology, 6*, 348. https://doi.org/10.3389/fpsyg.2015.00348

de Bono, E. (1985). *De Bono's thinking course*. London: Ariel Books.

de Jong, T. (2010). Cognitive load theory, educational research, and instructional design: Some food for thought. *Instructional Science, 38*(2), 105–134.

Dehaene, S. (2009). *Reading in the brain: The new science of how we read*. New York: Penguin.

Dehaene, S., & Cohen, L. (2011). The unique role of the visual word form area in reading. *Trends in Cognitive Sciences, 15*(6), 254–262. https://doi.org/10.1016 /j.tics.2011.04.003

Dehaene, S., Cohen, L., Morais, J., & Kolinsky, R. (2015). Illiterate to literate: Behavioural and cerebral changes induced by reading acquisition. *Nature Reviews Neuroscience, 16*(4), 234–244. https://doi.org/10.1038/nrn3924

Dehaene-Lambertz, G., Monzalvo, K., & Dehaene, S. (2018). The emergence of the visual word form: Longitudinal evolution of category-specific ventral visual areas during reading acquisition. *PloS Biology, 16*(3), 1–34. https://doi.org/10.1371/journal .pbio.2004103

Demb, J. B., Boynton, G. M., & Heeger, D. J. (1998). Functional magnetic resonance imaging of early visual pathways in dyslexia. *The Journal of Neuroscience, 18*(17), 6939–6951. https://doi.org/10.1523/JNEUROSCI.18-17-06939.1998

Demo, H., Nes, K., Somby, H. M., Frizzarin, A., & Dal Zovo, S. (2021). In and out of class—what is the meaning for inclusive schools? Teachers' opinions on push-in and pull-out in Italy and Norway. *International Journal of Inclusive Education*, 1–19. https://doi.org/10.1080/13603116.2021.1904017

Dessemontet, R. S., de Chambrier, A., Martinet, C., Moser, U., & Bayer, N. (2017). Exploring phonological awareness skills in children with intellectual disability. *American Journal on Intellectual and Developmental Disabilities, 122*(6), 476–491. https://doi.org/10.1352/1944-7558-122.6.476

Dessemontet, R. S., Martinet, C., de Chambrier, A.-F., Martini-Willemin, B.-M., & Audrin, C. (2019). A meta-analysis on the effectiveness of phonics instruction for teaching decoding skills to students with intellectual disability. *Educational Research Review, 26*, 52–70. https://doi.org/10.1016/j.edurev.2019.01.001

Dodge, K. A., Bierman, K. L., Coie, J. D., Greenberg, M. T., Lochman, J. E., McMahon, R. J., et al. (2015). Impact of early intervention on psychopathology, crime, and well-being at age 25. *The American Journal of Psychiatry, 172*(1), 59–70. https://doi.org/10.1176/appi.ajp.2014.13060786

Dole, J. A., & Nokes, J. D. (2009). Cognitive strategy instruction. In G. G. Duffy & S. E. Israel (Eds.), *Handbook of research on reading comprehension* (pp. 723–743). New York: Routledge.

Doll, B., & Cummings, J. A. (2007). *Transforming school mental health services: Population-based approaches to promoting the competency and wellness of children.* Thousand Oaks, CA: Corwin. Accessed at https://ebookcentral.proquest.com/lib/mcgill/reader.action?docID=1994150# on May 2, 2022.

Dougherty Stahl, K. A. (2016). Response to intervention: Is the sky falling? *The Reading Teacher, 69*(6), 659–663. https://doi.org/10.1002/trtr.1457

Drishti IAS. (2020, July 10). *World War II*. Drishti IAS. Accessed at https://www.drishtiias.com/to-the-points/paper1/world-war-ii#:~:text=The%20major%20causes%20of%20World,of%20the%20League%20of%20Nations on October 21, 2022.

Duque de Blas, G., Gómez-Veiga, I., & García-Madruga, J. A. (2021). Arithmetic word problems revisited: Cognitive processes and academic performance in secondary school. *Education Sciences, 11*(4), 155. https://doi.org/10.3390/educsci11040155

Durkin, D. (1993). *Teaching them to read* (6th ed.). New York: Allyn and Bacon.

Dwyer, E. J. (2001). *Learning words with common rimes.* Accessed at http://efaidnbmnnnibpcajpcglclefindmkaj/https://files.eric.ed.gov/fulltext/ED450407.pdf on June 23, 2023.

Dyslexia Reading Well. (n.d.). *The 44 sounds (phonemes) of English.* Accessed at www.dyslexia-reading-well.com/support-files/the-44-phonemes-of-english.pdf on October 25, 2023.

Earle, G. A., & Sayeski, K. L. (2017). Systematic instruction in phoneme-grapheme correspondence for students with reading disabilities. *Intervention in School and Clinic, 52*(5), 262–269. https://doi.org/10.1177/1053451216676798

Education Advisory Board. (n.d.). *Narrowing the third-grade reading gap: Embracing the science of reading.* District Leadership Forum. Accessed at https://www.idaontario.com/wp-content/uploads/2019/10/EAB-2019-Narrowing-the-Third-Grade-Reading-Gap_research-briefing.pdf on April 6, 2023.

Ehri, L. C. (2015). How children learn to read words. In A. Pollatsek and R. Treiman (Eds.), *The Oxford handbook of reading* (pp. 293–310). New York: Oxford University Press.

Ehri, L. C. (2022). What teachers need to know and do to teach letter–sounds, phonemic awareness, word reading, and phonics. *The Reading Teacher, 76*(1), 1–9. https://doi .org/10.1002/trtr.2095

Elliott, J. G., & Grigorenko, E. L. (2014). The end of dyslexia? *The Psychologist, 27*(8), 576–580.

Epler, P. L. (Ed.). (2017). *Instructional strategies in general education and putting the individuals with disabilities act (IDEA) into practice.* Hershey, PA: IGI Global.

Figurate, L. (n.d.). *Teaching vocabulary: Intentional, explicit instruction* [PowerPoint slides]. Dokumen. Accessed at https://dokumen.tips/documents/teaching-vocabulary-1. html?page=1 on April 6, 2023.

Finn, E. S., Shen, X., Holahan, J. M., Scheinost, D., Lacadie, C., Papademetris, X., et al. (2014). Disruption of functional networks in dyslexia: A whole-brain, data-driven analysis of connectivity. *Biological Psychiatry, 76*(5), 397–404. https://doi.org/10.1016 /j.biopsych.2013.08.031

Fisher, D., Frey, N., & Lapp, D. (2023). Veteran teachers' understanding of "balanced literacy," *Journal of Education, 203*(1), 188–195.

Fisher, D., Frey, N., Smith, D., & Hattie, J. (2021). *Rebound, grades K–12: A playbook for rebuilding agency, accelerating learning recovery, and rethinking schools.* Thousand Oaks, CA: Corwin.

Fisher, D., & Frey, N. (2021). Better learning through structured teaching: A framework for the gradual release of responsibility. Alexandria, VA: Association for Supervision and Curriculum Development.

Forey, G., & Cheung, L. M. E. (2019). The benefits of explicit teaching of language for curriculum learning in the physical education classroom. *English for Specific Purposes, 54*, 91–109. https://doi.org/10.1016/j.esp.2019.01.001

Frayer, D., Frederick, W. C., & Klausmeier, H. J. (1969). *A schema for testing the level of cognitive mastery.* Madison, WI: Wisconsin Center for Education Research.

Fusaroli, R., Weed, E., Fein, D., & Naigles, L. (2019). Hearing me hearing you: Reciprocal effects between child and parent language in autism and typical development. *Cognition, 183*, 1–18.

Gazith, K. (2021). *Teaching with purpose: How to thoughtfully implement evidence-based practices in your classroom.* Bloomington, IN: Solution Tree Press.

Genlott, A. A., & Grönlund, Å. (2013). Improving literacy skills through learning reading by writing: The iWTR method presented and tested. *Computers & Education, 67,* 98–104. https://doi.org/10.1016/j.compedu.2013.03.007

Gewertz, C. (2020, February 20). States to schools: Teach reading the right way. *Education Week.* Accessed at www.edweek.org/teaching-learning/states-to-schools-teach-reading -the-right-way/2020/02 on April 6, 2023.

Gillon, G. T. (2018). *Phonological awareness: From research to practice* (2nd ed.). New York: Guilford Press.

Golinkoff, R. M., Can, D. D., Soderstrom, M., & Hirsh-Pasek, K. (2015). (Baby)talk to me: The social context of infant-directed speech and its effects on early language acquisition. *Current Directions in Psychological Science, 24*(5), 339–344. https://doi .org/10.1177/0963721415595345

Goswami, U. C., & Bryant, P. (2016). *Phonological skills and learning to read.* New York: Routledge.

Gough, P. B., & Tunmer, W. E. (1986). Decoding, reading, and reading disability. *Remedial and Special Education, 7*(1), 6–10.

Graesser, A. C., Cai, Z., Baer, W. O., Olney, A. M., Hu, X., Reed, M., et al. (2016). Reading comprehension lessons in AutoTutor for the Center for the Study of Adult Literacy. In S. A. Crossley & D. S. McNamara (Eds.), *Adaptive educational technologies for literacy instruction* (pp. 288–293). New York: Routledge.

Greene, J. P. (1997). A meta-analysis of the Rossell and Baker review of bilingual education research. *Bilingual Research Journal, 21*(2–3), 103–122. https://doi.org/10.1080/1523 5882.1997.10668656

Grillo, K. J., & Dieker, L. A. (2013). A new twist on vocabulary instruction for students with learning disabilities in biology. *The American Biology Teacher, 75*(4), 264–267. https://doi.org/10.1525/abt.2013.75.4.7

Grofčíková, S., & Máčajová, M. (2021). Rhyming in the context of the phonological awareness of pre-school children. *Center for Educational Policy Studies Journal, 11*(1), 115–138. https://doi.org/10.26529/cepsj.685

Guilmois, C., Popa-Roch, M., Clément, C., Bissonnette, S., & Troadec, B. (2019). Effective numeracy educational interventions for students from disadvantaged social background: A comparison of two teaching methods. *Educational Research and Evaluation, 25*(7–8), 336–356. https://doi.org/10.1080/13803611.2020.1830119

Harvey, S., & Goudvis, A. (2007). *Strategies that work: Teaching comprehension for understanding and engagement.* Portsmouth, NH: Stenhouse.

Hasbrouck, J. (2006). Drop everything and read—but how? For students who are not yet fluent, silent reading is not the best use of classroom time. *American Educator, 30*(2), 22–31. Accessed at https://www.aft.org/periodical/american-educator/summer-2006/drop-everything-and-read-how on April 10, 2023.

Hasbrouck, J., & Tindal, G. (2017). *An update to compiled ORF norms* (Technical Report No. 1702). Eugene, OR: Behavioral Research and Teaching. Accessed at https://files.eric.ed.gov/fulltext/ED594994.pdf on April 10, 2023.

Hattie, J. (2012). *Visible learning for teachers: Maximizing impact on learning.* New York: Routledge/Taylor & Francis Group. https://doi.org/10.4324/9780203181522

Hattie, J., & Zierer, K. (2019). *Visible learning insights.* New York: Routledge.

Hayes, D. A., & Tierney, R. J. (1980). *Increasing background knowledge through analogy: Its effects upon comprehension and learning* (Report No. 186). Center for the Study of Reading. Accessed at https://files.eric.ed.gov/fulltext/ED195953.pdf on April 10, 2023.

Helman, A. L., Calhoon, M. B., & Kern, L. (2015). Improving science vocabulary of high school English language learners with reading disabilities. *Learning Disability Quarterly, 38*(1), 40–52. https://doi.org/10.1177/0731948714539769

Hempenstall, K. (2009). Research-driven reading assessment: Drilling to the core. *Australian Journal of Learning Difficulties, 14*(1), 17–52. https://doi.org/10.1080/19404150902783419

Hempenstall, K. (2013). *Literacy assessment based upon the National Reading Panel's big five components.* National Institute for Direct Instruction. [Blog post]. Accessed at https://www.nifdi.org/newsite/resources/hempenstall-blog/393-literacy-assessment-based-upon-the-national-reading-panel-s-big-five-components.html on April 10, 2023.

Hicks, D., Doolittle, P. E., & Ewing, E. T. (2004). The SCIM-C strategy: Expert historians, historical inquiry, and multimedia. *Social Education, 68*(3), 221–226.

Hinshelwood, J. (1900, 26 May). Congenital word-blindness. *The Lancet, 155*(4004), 1506–1508.

Hoover, W. A., & Tunmer, W. E. (2018). The simple view of reading: Three assessments of its adequacy. *Remedial and Special Education, 39*(5), 304–312. https://doi.org/10.1177/0741932518773154

Hornickel, J., & Kraus, N. (2013). Unstable representation of sound: A biological marker of dyslexia. *Journal of Neuroscience, 33*(8), 3500–3504. https://doi.org/10.1523/JNEUROSCI.4205-12.2013

Hougen, M. (2016, July). *Phonemic awareness: The single sound challenge.* Language Arts for Young Children. Accessed at https://courses.lumenlearning.com/hostos-edu104/chapter/phonemic-awareness/ on April 10, 2023.

Ibrahim, E. H. E., Sarudin, I., & Muhamad, A. J. (2016). The relationship between vocabulary size and reading comprehension of ESL learners. *English Language Teaching, 9*(2), 116–123.

Ijalba, E., & Obler, L. K. (2015). *First language grapheme-phoneme transparency effects in adult second-language learning.* ScholarSpace. Accessed at http://hdl.handle.net /10125/66700 on April 10, 2023.

International Dyslexia Association. (2020). *Dyslexia and the brain* [Fact sheet]. Accessed at https://dyslexiaida.org/dyslexia-and-the-brain/ on April 10, 2023.

Itchy's Alphabet. (n.d.). *Teaching children to read with phonics games.* Accessed at https:// itchysalphabet.com on April 12, 2023.

Jing, L., Vermeire, K., Mangino, A., & Reuterskiöld, C. (2019). Rhyme awareness in children with normal hearing and children with cochlear implants: An exploratory study. *Frontiers in Psychology, 10.* Accessed at https://www.frontiersin.org/article /10.3389/fpsyg.2019.02072 on April 10, 2023.

Johnston, P. H. (2011). Response to intervention in literacy: Problems and possibilities. *The Elementary School Journal, 111*(4), 511–534.

Justice, L. M., & Sofka, A. E. (2010). *Engaging children with print: Building early literacy skills through quality read-alouds.* New York: Guilford Press.

Kaczmarek, B. (2020). Current views on neuroplasticity: What is new and what is old? *Acta Neuropsychologica, 18*, 1–14.

Kaplan Test Prep. (n.d.). *GMAT reading comprehension practice: Difficult passages.* Accessed at www.kaptest.com/study/gmat/high-level-gmat-reading-comprehension-practice on June 26, 2023.

Kang, E. Y., & Shin, M. (2019). The contributions of reading fluency and decoding to reading comprehension for struggling readers in fourth grade. *Reading & Writing Quarterly, 35*(3), 179–192. https://doi.org/10.1080/10573569.2018.1521758

Kannings, A. (2014). *Vince Lombardi: His words.* Morrisville, NC: Lulu Press.

Katiyar, S. P. (2021). Adult illiteracy: A global social problem. In R. Baikady, S. M. Sajid, J. Przeperski, V. Nadesan, I. Rezaul, & J. Gao (Eds.), *The Palgrave handbook of global social problems* (pp. 1–20). New York: Springer International Publishing.

Keene, E. O., & Zimmermann, S. (2007). *Mosaic of thought: The power of comprehension strategy instruction* (2nd ed.). Portsmouth, NH: Heinemann.

Kemp, K. (2016). *180 days of problem solving for third grade.* Huntington Beach, CA: Shell Educational Publishing.

Kent State University. (n.d.). *Three level comprehension guide for active reading*. Kent, OH: Author. Accessed at https://www.kent.edu/writingcommons/three-level -comprehension-guide-active-reading on April 12, 2023.

Kilpatrick, D. A., Joshi, R. M., & Wagner, R. K. (2019). *Reading development and difficulties: Bridging the gap between research and practice*. New York: Springer Nature.

Kim, S. Y., & Cao, F. (2022). How does the brain read different scripts? Evidence from English, Korean, and Chinese. *Reading and Writing, 35*(6), 1449–1473. https://doi .org/10.1007/s11145-022-10263-9

Kirby, P. (2020). Dyslexia debated, then and now: A historical perspective on the dyslexia debate. *Oxford Review of Education, 46*(4), 472–486. https://doi.org/10.1080/030549 85.2020.1747418

Klages, C., Scholtens, M.-M., Fowler, K., & Frierson, C. (2020). Linking science-based research with a structured literacy program to teach students with dyslexia to read: Connections: OG in 3-D®. *Reading Improvement, 57*(2), 47–57.

Kosanovich, M. L., Reed, D. K., & Miller, D. H. (2010). *Bringing literacy strategies into content instruction: Professional learning for secondary-level teachers*. Portsmouth, NH: Center on Instruction. Accessed at https://files.eric.ed.gov/fulltext/ED521883.pdf on April 10, 2023.

Kovelman, L., Bisconti, S., & Hoeft, F. (2016, April). *Literacy & dyslexia revealed through bilingual brain development*. Pikesville, MD: International Dyslexia Association. Accessed at https://dyslexiaida.org/literacy-dyslexia-revealed-through-bilingual-brain -development/ on April 10, 2023.

Krafnick, A. J., Tan, L.-H., Flowers, D. L., Luetje, M. M., Napoliello, E. M., Siok, W.-T., et al. (2016). Chinese character and English word processing in children's ventral occipitotemporal cortex: fMRI evidence for script invariance. *NeuroImage, 133*, 302–312.

Kulkarni, S. S., Parmar, J., Selmi, A., & Mendelson, A. (2019). Assistive technology for students with disabilities: An international and intersectional approach. In A. H. Normore & A. I. Lahera (Eds.), *Crossing the bridge of the digital divide: A walk with global leaders* (pp. 197–208). Charlotte, NC: Information Age.

Kwok, E. Y. L., Brown, H. M., Smyth, R. E., & Cardy, J. O. (2015). Meta-analysis of receptive and expressive language skills in autism spectrum disorder. *Research in Autism Spectrum Disorders, 9*, 202–222. https://doi.org/10.1016/j.rasd.2014.10.008

Learning Disabilities Association of America. (2015). *Adults with learning disabilities: An overview* [Info sheet]. Accessed at https://ldaamerica.org/info/adults-with-learning- disabilities-an-overview/ on April 10, 2023.

Lee, J., & Yoon, S. Y. (2017). The effects of repeated reading on reading fluency for students with reading disabilities: A meta-analysis. *Journal of Learning Disabilities, 50*(2), 213–224. https://doi.org/10.1177/0022219415605194

Leighton Gamel, A. (2015). *Help! My college students can't read: Teaching vital reading strategies in the content areas.* New York: Rowman & Littlefield.

León, J. A., & Escudero, I. (2015). Understanding causality in science discourse for middle and high school students: Summary task as a strategy for improving comprehension. In K. L. Santi & D. K. Reed (Eds.), *Improving reading comprehension of middle and high school students* (Vol. 10, pp. 75–98). New York: Springer.

Let's Talk Science. (2019, August 21). *What is mitosis?* Accessed at https://letstalkscience.ca/educational-resources/backgrounders/what-mitosis on April 10, 2023.

Lewis, M. (2002). *The lexical approach: The state of ELT and a way forward.* Stamford, CT: Thomson Corporation.

Linkersdörfer, J., Jurcoane, A., Lindberg, S., Kaiser, J., Hasselhorn, M., Fiebach, C. J., & Lonnemann, J. (2015). The association between gray matter volume and reading proficiency: A longitudinal study of beginning readers. *Journal of Cognitive Neuroscience, 27*(2), 308–318. https://doi.org/10.1162/jocn_a_00710

Literacy Connects. (n.d.). *The big 5: Key concepts for learning to read.* Accessed at https://literacyconnects.org/pdfs/The-Big-5-Explanations-of-Reading-Concepts.pdf on October 25, 2023.

Littky, D. (2004). *The big picture: Education is everyone's business.* Alexandria, VA: ASCD.

López-Barroso, D., de Schotten, M. T., Morais, J., Kolinsky, R., Braga, L. W., Guerreiro-Tauil, A., et al. (2020). Impact of literacy on the functional connectivity of vision and language related networks. *NeuroImage, 213*, Article 116722. https://doi.org/10.1016/j.neuroimage.2020.116722

Lovett, M. W., Frijters, J. C., Wolf, M., Steinbach, K. A., Sevcik, R. A., & Morris, R. D. (2017). Early intervention for children at risk for reading disabilities: The impact of grade at intervention and individual differences on intervention outcomes. *Journal of Educational Psychology, 109*(7), 889–914. https://doi.org/10.1037/edu0000181

Lupo, S. M., Hardigree, C., Thacker, E. S., Sawyer, A. G., & Merritt, J. D. (2022). *Teaching disciplinary literacy in grades K–6: Infusing content with reading, writing, and language.* New York: Routledge.

Martiniello, M. (2008). Language and the performance of English-language learners in math word problems. *Harvard Educational Review, 78*(2), 333–368. https://doi.org/10.17763/haer.78.2.70783570r1111t32

Martin-Kniep, G., & Picone-Zocchia, J. (2009). *Changing the way you teach, improving the way students learn.* Alexandria, VA: ASCD.

Marinelli, C. V., Romani, C., Burani, C., & Zoccolotti, P. (2015). Spelling acquisition in English and Italian: A cross-linguistic study. *Frontiers in Psychology, 6*, Article 1843. https://doi.org/10.3389/fpsyg.2015.01843

Marzano, R. J. (2017). *The new art and science of teaching.* Bloomington, IN: Solution Tree Press & ASCD.

Massey, D. D. (2015). Reading history: Moving from memorizing facts to critical thinking. In K. L. Santi & D. K. Reed (Eds.), *Improving reading comprehension of middle and high school students* (Vol. 10, pp. 19–48). New York: Springer.

McArthur, G., Sheehan, Y., Badcock, N. A., Francis, D. A., Wang, H.-C., Kohnen, S., et al. (2018). Phonics training for English-speaking poor readers. *Cochrane Database of Systematic Reviews,* (11). https://doi.org/10.1002/14651858.CD009115.pub3

McKnight, K. S. (2014). *Common core literacy for ELA, history/social studies, and the humanities: Strategies to deepen content knowledge (grades 6–12).* San Francisco: Jossey-Bass.

McMaster, K. L., Espin, C. A., & van den Broek, P. (2014). Making connections: Linking cognitive psychology and intervention research to improve comprehension of struggling readers. *Learning Disabilities Research & Practice, 29*(1), 17–24. https://doi.org/10.1111/ldrp.12026

McNorgan, C. (2021). The connectivity fingerprints of highly-skilled and disordered reading persist across cognitive domains. *Frontiers in Computational Neuroscience, 15,* Article 590093. https://doi.org/10.3389/fncom.2021.590093

Milankov, V., Golubović, S., Krstić, T., & Golubović, Š. (2021). Phonological awareness as the foundation of reading acquisition in students reading in transparent orthography. *International Journal of Environmental Research and Public Health, 18*(10), 5440. https://doi.org/10.3390/ijerph18105440

Missall, K. N., Hosp, M. K., & Hosp, J. L. (2019). Reading proficiency in elementary: Considering statewide testing, teacher ratings and rankings, and reading curriculum-based measurement. *School Psychology Review, 48*(3), 267–275. https://doi.org/10.17105/SPR-2017-0152.V48-3

Moats, L. (2007). *Whole-language high jinks: How to tell when "scientifically-based reading instruction" isn't.* Washington, DC: Thomas B. Fordham Institute. Accessed at https://files.eric.ed.gov/fulltext/ED498005.pdf on April 10, 2023.

Moats, L. C. (2020). Teaching reading is rocket science: What expert teachers of reading should know and be able to do. *American Educator, 44*(2). Accessed at https://www.aft.org/ae/summer2020/moats on April 10, 2023.

Moghadam, S. H., Zainal, Z., & Ghaderpour, M. (2012). A review on the important role of vocabulary knowledge in reading comprehension performance. *Procedia—Social and Behavioral Sciences, 66,* 555–563. https://doi.org/10.1016/j.sbspro.2012.11.300

Moje, E., Stockdill, D., Kim, K., & Kim, H. (2011). The role of text in disciplinary learning. In M. Kamil, P. Pearson, E. Moje, & P. Afflerbach (Eds.), *Handbook of reading research* (Vol. IV, pp. 453–486). New York, NY: Routledge.

Moodie-Reid, L. (2016). *Teachers' perceptions of the impact of the jolly phonics program on students' literacy* (Publication No. 10024534) [Doctoral dissertation, Walden University]. ProQuest Dissertations & Theses. Accessed at https://www.proquest.com/docview/1770078064 on April 10, 2023.

Moore v. British Columbia (Education), SCC 61, 3 SCR 360 (2012). Accessed at https://scc-csc.lexum.com/scc-csc/scc-csc/en/item/12680/index.do on April 10, 2023.

Morgan, M. (2016, April 27). *Dr. Anita Archer: Vocabulary development 2/03.* Silo Tips. Accessed at https://silo.tips/download/dr-anita-archer-vocabulary-development-2-03 on April 10, 2023.

Muijs, D., & Reynolds, D. (2018). *Effective teaching: Evidence and practice* (4th ed.). Thousand Oaks, CA: SAGE.

Mulcahey, M. A. (2018, January 17). What does it mean to be "on the bubble" in an academic skill? Cincinnati, OH: Springer School & Center. Accessed at https://www.springer-ld.org/2018/01/17/what-does-it-mean-to-be-on-the-bubble-in-an-academic-skill/#:~:text=A%20child%20who%20is%20%E2%80%9Con,the%20cutoff%20by%20one%20point on April 12, 2023.

Narayan, C. R., & McDermott, L. C. (2016). Speech rate and pitch characteristics of infant-directed speech: Longitudinal and cross-linguistic observations. *The Journal of the Acoustical Society of America, 139*(3), 1272–1281. https://doi.org/10.1121/1.4944634

Nation, K. (2019). Children's reading difficulties, language, and reflections on the simple view of reading. *Australian Journal of Learning Difficulties, 24*(1), 47–73. https://doi.org/10.1080/19404158.2019.1609272

National Assessment of Educational Progress. (2017). *The nation's report card: Mathematics & reading.* Washington, DC: U.S. Government Printing Office. Accessed at www.nationsreportcard.gov on August 22, 2023.

National Assessment of Educational Progress. (2022). *NAEP report card: Reading.* Accessed at https://www.nationsreportcard.gov/reading/nation/achievement/?grade=8 on April 12, 2023.

National Center for Education Statistics. (n.d.). *Fast facts: Adult literacy.* Accessed at https://nces.ed.gov/fastfacts/display.asp?id=69 on May 2, 2022.

National Geographic. (n.d.). *Jun 28, 1919 CE: Treaty of Versailles.* Accessed at https://education.nationalgeographic.org/resource/treaty-versailles-ends-wwi on April 6, 2023.

National Institute of Child Health and Human Development & U.S. Department of Education. (2000). *Teaching children to read: An evidence-based assessment of the scientific research literature on reading and its implications for reading instruction.* Accessed at https://www.nichd.nih.gov/sites/default/files/publications/pubs/nrp /Documents/report.pdf on April 12, 2023.

National Reading Panel. (2000). *Teaching children to read: An evidence-based assessment of the scientific literature.* Washington, DC: National Institute of Child Health and Human Development.

Nijhof, A. D., & Willems, R. M. (2015). Simulating fiction: Individual differences in literature comprehension revealed with fMRI. *PloS One, 10*(2), Article e0116492. https://doi.org/10.1371/journal.pone.0116492

NSW Department of Education and Training. (2009). *Literacy teaching guide: Phonics.* Parramatta, New South Wales, Australia: Author. Accessed at https://my.vanderbilt. edu/specialeducationinduction/files/2011/09/1-Literacy -teaching-guide-phonics.pdf on April 10, 2023.

Ontario Human Rights Commission. (2022). *Right to read: Public inquiry into human rights issues affecting students with reading disabilities.* Toronto, Ontario, Canada: Author. Accessed at https://www.ohrc.on.ca/en/right-to-read-inquiry-report on April 12, 2023.

Ortlieb, E., & Cheek, E. H., Jr. (Eds.). (2013). *School-based interventions for struggling readers, K–8.* Bingley, England: Emerald Group Publishing.

Osborn, J., & Lehr, F. (2003). *A focus on fluency. Research-based practices in early reading series.* Honolulu, HI: Pacific Resources for Education and Learning (PREL). Accessed at https://eric.ed.gov/?id=ED481962 on June 23, 2023.

Oczkus, L. D. (2018). *Reciprocal teaching at work: Powerful strategies and lessons for improving reading comprehension.* Alexandria, VA: ASCD.

Palincsar, A., & Brown, A. L. (1984). Reciprocal teaching of comprehension-fostering and monitoring activities. *Cognition and Instruction, 1*(2), 117–175. https://doi .org/10.1207/s1532690xci0102_1

Panagouli, E., Stavridou, A., Savvidi, C., Kourti, A., Psaltopoulou, T., Sergentanis, T.N., & Tsitsika, A. (2021). School performance among children and adolescents during COVID-19 pandemic: A systematic review. *Children, 8*(12), Article 12.

Pavlov, I.P. (1927). *Conditioned reflexes.* Oxford, England: Oxford University Press.

Pearson, P. D., & Dole, J. A. (1987). Explicit comprehension instruction: A review of research and a new conceptualization of instruction. *The Elementary School Journal, 88*(2), 151–165. https://doi.org/10.1086/461530

Pearson, P. D., & Gallagher, M. C. (1983). The instruction of reading comprehension. *Contemporary Educational Psychology, 8*(3), 317–344.

Pennsylvania Training and Technical Assistance Network. (n.d.). *RTI/SLD determination.* Accessed at https://www.pattan.net/Multi-Tiered-System-of-Support/Response-to-Intervention-RTI/RTI-SLD-Determination on April 12, 2023.

Pepper Rollins, S. (2014). *Learning in the fast lane: 8 ways to put ALL students on the road to academic success.* Alexandria, VA: ASCD.

Pilten, G. (2016). The evaluation of effectiveness of reciprocal teaching strategies on comprehension of expository texts. *Journal of Education and Training Studies, 4*(10), 232–247.

Pinker, S. (2009). *Language learnability and language development: With new commentary by the author.* Cambridge, MA: Harvard University Press.

Price, K. W., Meisinger, E. B., Louwerse, M. M., & D'Mello, S. (2016). The contributions of oral and silent reading fluency to reading comprehension. *Reading Psychology, 37*(2), 167–201.

Primary National Strategy. (2006). *Phonics and early reading: An overview for headteachers, literacy leaders and teachers in schools, and managers and practitioners in Early Years settings.* London, UK: Department of Education and Skills. Accessed at https://dera.ioe.ac.uk/id/eprint/5551/3/5d970d28fc535dc54eb4dee9995bef36.pdf on April 12, 2023.

Programme for International Student Assessment [PISA]. (2018). Highlights of U.S. PISA 2018 Results Web Report (NCES 2020–166 and NCES 2020–072). U.S. Department of Education. Institute of Education Sciences, National Center for Education Statistics. Accessed at https://nces.ed.gov/surveys/pisa/pisa2018/index.asp on April 10, 2023.

Pugh, K. R., Frost, S. J., Rothman, D. L., Hoeft, F., Del Tufo, S. N., Mason, G. F., et al. (2014). Glutamate and choline levels predict individual differences in reading ability in emergent readers. *Journal of Neuroscience, 34*(11), 4082–4089. https://doi.org/10.1523/JNEUROSCI.3907-13.2014

Pugh, K. R., Mencl, W. E., Jenner, A. R., Katz, L., Frost, S. J., Lee, J. R., et al. (2001). Neurobiological studies of reading and reading disability. *Journal of Communication Disorders, 34*(6), 479–492. https://doi.org/10.1016/S0021-9924(01)00060-0

Quigley, A. (2020). *Closing the reading gap.* New York: Routledge.

Rahul, D. R., & Ponniah, R. J. (2021). The modularity of dyslexia. *Pediatrics & Neonatology, 62*(3), 240–248.

Raschle, N. M., Zuk, J., & Gaab, N. (2012). Functional characteristics of developmental dyslexia in left-hemispheric posterior brain regions predate reading onset. *PNAS Proceedings of the National Academy of Sciences of the United States of America, 109*(6), 2156–2161. https://doi.org/10.1073/pnas.1107721109

Rasinski, T. V., Rupley, W. H., Pagie, D. D., & Nichols, W. D. (2016). Alternative text types to improve reading fluency for competent to struggling readers. *International Journal of Instruction, 9*(1), 163–178.

Read Naturally. (n.d.) *Phonics*. Accessed at https://www.readnaturally.com/research/5-components-of-reading/phonics on April 12, 2023.

Reading, S., & Van Deuren, D. (2007). Phonemic awareness: When and how much to teach? *Reading Research and Instruction, 46*(3), 267–285.

Reading Rockets. (n.d.a). *Assessment: In depth*. Accessed at www.readingrockets.org/teaching/reading101-course/modules/assessment/assessment-depth on May 2, 2022.

Reading Rockets. (n.d.b.). *Phonics: In practice*. Accessed at https://www.readingrockets.org/teaching/reading101-course/modules/phonics/phonics-practice on August 10, 2022.

Reading Rockets. (2019, January 25). *What is the dyslexia paradox?* [Video file]. Accessed at https://www.youtube.com/watch?v=GEbTEt1HHNE&list=PLLxDwKxHx1yKu1grW2KBgvRnPltqkD01S on April 12, 2023.

Reid, G. (2016). *Dyslexia: A practitioner's handbook* (5th ed.). Hoboken, NJ: Wiley.

Restori, A. F., Katz, G. S., & Lee, H. B. (2009). A critique of the IQ/achievement discrepancy model for identifying specific learning disabilities. *Europe's Journal of Psychology, 5*(4), 128–145. https://doi.org/10.5964/ejop.v5i4.244

Reutzel, D. R., Child, A., Jones, C. D., & Clark, S. K. (2014). Explicit instruction in core reading programs. *The Elementary School Journal, 114*(3), 406–430. https://doi.org/10.1086/674420

Riccomini, P. J., Smith, G. W., Hughes, E. M., & Fries, K. M. (2015). The language of mathematics: The importance of teaching and learning mathematical vocabulary. *Reading & Writing Quarterly, 31*(3), 235–252. https://doi.org/10.1080/10573569.2015.1030995

Rolstad, K., Mahoney, K. S., & Glass, G. V. (2005). Weighing the evidence: A meta-analysis of bilingual education in Arizona. *Bilingual Research Journal, 29*(1), 43–67. https://doi.org/10.1080/15235882.2005.10162823

Romeo, R. R., Segaran, J., Leonard, J. A., Robinson, S. T., West, M. R., Mackey, A. P., et al. (2018). Language exposure relates to structural neural connectivity in childhood. *Journal of Neuroscience, 38*(36), 7870–7877. https://doi.org/10.1523/JNEUROSCI.0484-18.2018

Roosevelt, F. D. (1933, March 12). *Fireside chat 1: On the banking crisis*. Accessed at https://millercenter.org/the-presidency/presidential-speeches/march-12-1933-fireside -chat-1-banking-crisis on April 12, 2023.

Rothman, R. (1990, March 21). From a "great debate" to a full-scale war: Dispute over teaching reading heats up. *Education Week*. Accessed at www.edweek.org/teaching -learning/from-a-great-debate-to-a-full-scale-war-dispute-over-teaching-reading -heats-up/1990/03 on June 23, 2023.

Rupley, W. H., Blair, T. R., & Nichols, W. D. (2009). Effective reading instruction for struggling readers: The role of direct/explicit teaching. *Reading & Writing Quarterly*, *25*(2–3), 125–138. https://doi.org/10.1080/10573560802683523

Santi, K. L., & Reed, D. K. (Eds.). (2015). *Improving reading comprehension of middle and high school students* (Vol. 10). New York: Springer.

Sayeski, K. L., Earle, G. A., Eslinger, R. P., & Whitenton, J. N. (2017). Teacher candidates' mastery of phoneme-grapheme correspondence: Massed versus distributed practice in teacher education. *Annals of Dyslexia*, *67*(1), 26–41.

Scanlon, D., & Baker, D. (2012). An accommodations model for the secondary inclusive classroom. *Learning Disability Quarterly*, *35*(4), 212–224. https://doi. org/10.1177/0731948712451261

Schaars, M. M. H., Segers, E., & Verhoeven, L. (2017). Predicting the integrated development of word reading and spelling in the early primary grades. *Learning and Individual Differences*, *59*, 127–140. https://doi.org/10.1016/j.lindif.2017.09.006

Schmitt, N., Jiang, X., & Grabe, W. (2011). The percentage of words known in a text and reading comprehension. *The Modern Language Journal*, *95*(1), 26–43.

Shanahan, T., & Shanahan, C. (2008). Teaching disciplinary literacy to adolescents: Rethinking content-area literacy. *Harvard Educational Review*, *78*(1), 40–59. https:// doi.org/10.17763/haer.78.1.v62444321p602101

Shaywitz, S. E., & Shaywitz, B. A. (2005). Dyslexia (specific reading disability). *Biological Psychiatry*, *57*(11), 1301–1309. https://doi.org/10.1016/j.biopsych.2005.01.043

Shaywitz, S. E., Morris, R., & Shaywitz, B. A. (2008). The education of dyslexic children from childhood to young adulthood. *Annual Review of Psychology*, *59*(1), 451–475.

Shaywitz, S. E., & Shaywitz, B. A. (2016). Reading disability and the brain. *On developing readers: Readings from educational leadership (EL essentials)*. Alexandria, VA: ASCD, 146–151.

Shaywitz, B. A., & Shaywitz, S. E. (2020). The American experience: Towards a 21st century definition of dyslexia. *Oxford Review of Education*, *46*(4), 454–471. https:// doi.org/10.1080/03054985.2020.1793545

Shaywitz, S. E., & Shaywitz, B. A. (2008). Paying attention to reading: The neurobiology of reading and dyslexia. *Development and Psychopathology, 20*(4), 1329–1349. https://doi.org/10.1017/S0954579408000631

Shaywitz, S. E., Shaywitz, J. E., & Shaywitz, B. A. (2021). Dyslexia in the 21st century. *Current Opinion in Psychiatry, 34*(2), 80–86. https://doi.org/10.1097/YCO.0000000000000670

Shinohara, K., & Wobbrock, J. O. (2011). In the shadow of misperception: Assistive technology use and social interactions. *Proceedings of the SIGCHI Conference on Human Factors in Computing Systems*, 705–714. https://doi.org/10.1145/1978942.1979044

Skill. (n.d.). In *Oxford learner's dictionaries*. Accessed at www.oxfordlearnersdictionaries.com/definition/american_english/skill on April 12, 2023.

Skinner, B. F. (1938). *The behaviour of organisms: An experimental analysis.* New York: Appleton-Century.

Smith, N. L., & Williams, B. K. (2020). Supporting middle school language arts teachers through professional development. *Reading Psychology, 41*(5), 403–419. https://doi.org/10.1080/02702711.2020.1768984

Smith, J. L. M., Sáez, L., & Doabler, C. T. (2016). Using explicit and systematic instruction to support working memory. *TEACHING Exceptional Children, 48*(6), 275–281. https://doi.org/10.1177/0040059916650633

Spiro, R. J., & Myers, A. (1984). Individual differences and underlying cognitive processes. In P. David Pearson (Ed.), *Handbook of reading research* (Vol. 1, pp. 471–501). New York: Routledge.

Sprenger, M. (2013). *Wiring the brain for reading: Brain-based strategies for teaching literacy.* San Francisco, CA: Jossey-Bass.

Statistics Canada. (2015, June 22). *Literacy, numeracy—Average scores and distribution of proficiency levels, by labour force status, highest level of education and age group.* Accessed at https://www150.statcan.gc.ca/t1/tbl1/en/tv.action?pid=3710004901 on April 12, 2023.

Stockard, J., Wood, T. W., Coughlin, C., & Rasplica Khoury, C. (2018). The effectiveness of direct instruction curricula: A meta-analysis of a half century of research. *Review of Educational Research, 88*(4), 479–507. https://doi.org/10.3102/0034654317751919

Strasser, K., Vergara, D., & del Río, M. F. (2017). Contributions of print exposure to first and second grade oral language and reading in Chile. *Journal of Research in Reading, 40*(S1), S87–S106. https://doi.org/10.1111/1467-9817.12086

Swanson, E., Barnes, M., Fall, A.-M., & Roberts, G. (2018). Predictors of reading comprehension among struggling readers who exhibit differing levels of inattention and hyperactivity. *Reading & Writing Quarterly: Overcoming Learning Difficulties, 34*(2), 132–146.

Sweet, R. W. (2004). The big picture: Where we are nationally on the reading front and how we got there. In P. McCardle & V. Chhabra (Eds.), *The voice of evidence in reading research* (pp. 13–44). Baltimore: Brookes Publishing.

Yale Center for Dyslexia & Creativity. (2017). Video from the House Committee hearing on "The Science of Dyslexia." [Video]. Accessed at https://dyslexia.yale.edu/video -from-the-house-committee-hearing-onthe-science-of-dyslexia/ on April 12, 2023.

Torgesen, J. K. (2004). Lessons learned from research on interventions for students who have difficulty learning to read. In P. McCardle & V. Chhabra (Eds.), *The voice of evidence in reading research* (pp. 355–382). Baltimore: Brookes Publishing.

Torgerson, C., Brooks, G., Gascoine, L., & Higgins, S. (2019). Phonics: Reading policy and the evidence of effectiveness from a systematic "tertiary" review. *Research Papers in Education, 34*(2), 208–238.

Toste, J. R., & Ciullo, S. (2017). Reading and writing instruction in the upper elementary grades. *Intervention in School and Clinic, 52*(5), 259–261.

Toste, J. R., Didion, L., Peng, P., Filderman, M. J., & McClelland, A. M. (2020). A meta-analytic review of the relations between motivation and reading achievement for K–12 students. *Review of Educational Research, 90*(3), 420–456.

Townsend, T. (2007). *International handbook of school effectiveness and improvement: Review, reflection and reframing.* New York: Springer.

Toy Theater. (n.d.). Elkolin boxes [Illustration]. Accessed at https://toytheater.com/ elkonin-boxes/ on April 12, 2023.

Treiman, R., Rosales, N., & Kessler, B. (2016). Characteristics of print in books for preschool children. *Writing Systems Research, 8*(1), 120–132. https://doi.org/10.1080 /17586801.2015.1074058

University College London. (2013, April 18). Learning disabilities affect up to 10 percent of children. *ScienceDaily.* Accessed at www.sciencedaily.com/releases/2013/04 /130418142309.htm on May 9, 2022.

University of Oregon. (n.d.). *What is DIBELS?* DIBELS: Dynamic Indicators of Basic Early Literacy Skills. Accessed at https://dibels.uoregon.edu/about-dibels on May 9, 2022.

University of Texas Center for Reading & Language Arts & Texas Education Agency. (2001). *Essential reading strategies for the struggling reader: Activities for an accelerated reading program.* Austin, TX: University of Texas System/Texas Education Agency. Accessed at https://content.schoolinsites.com/api/documents/a929f9c01112471 c9bedcee824ad7927.pdf on April 12, 2023.

Urquhart, V., & Frazee, D. (2012). *Teaching reading in the content areas: If not me, then who?* (3rd ed.). Alexandria, VA: ASCD.

VanSledright, B. A. (2004). What does it mean to teach historically and how do you teach it? *Social Education, 68*(3), 230–233.

Vardy, E. J., Al Otaiba, S., Breadmore, H. L., Kung, S.-H., Pétursdóttir, A.-L., Zaru, M. W., et al. (2022). Teacher–researcher partnership in the translation and implementing of PALS (Peer-Assisted Learning Strategies): An international perspective. *Journal of Research in Reading, 45*(3), 517–526. https://doi.org/10.1111/1467-9817.12404

Venema, G. (2006). *The foundations of geometry.* Hoboken, NJ: Pearson Prentice Hall.

Vocabulary. (n.d.). In Merriam-Webster's online dictionary. Accessed at https://www.merriam-webster.com/dictionary/vocabulary on May 23, 2022.

Vouglanis, T., & Driga, A. M. (2023). Educating students with dyslexia through ICT during the COVID-19 pandemic. *TechHub Journal, 5,* 20–33.

Vygotsky, L. S. (1978). *Mind in society: The development of higher psychological processes.* Cambridge, MA: Harvard University Press.

Wilfong, L. G. (2019). *Content area literacy strategies that work: Do this, not that!* New York: Routledge.

Wanzek, J., Wexler, J., Vaughn, S., & Ciullo, S. (2010). Reading interventions for struggling readers in the upper elementary grades: A synthesis of 20 years of research. *Reading and Writing, 23*(8), 889–912.

Wanzek, J., Stevens, E. A., Williams, K. J., Scammacca, N., Vaughn, S., & Sargent, K. (2018). Current evidence on the effects of intensive early reading interventions. *Journal of Learning Disabilities, 51*(6), 612–624. https://doi.org/10.1177/0022219418775110

Wanzek, J., Vaughn, S., Scammacca, N. K., Metz, K., Murray, C. S., Roberts, G., et al. (2013). Extensive reading interventions for students with reading difficulties after grade 3. *Review of Educational Research, 83*(2), 163–195.

Watkins, P. (2013). By teachers, for teachers. *English Teaching Professional,* 84.

Widdowson, H. G. (1989). Knowledge of language and ability for use. *Applied Linguistics, 10*(2), 128–137.

Wilkins, D. A. (1972). *Linguistics in language teaching.* London: Edward Arnold.

Williams, V. J., Juranek, J., Cirino, P., & Fletcher, J. M. (2018). Cortical thickness and local gyrification in children with developmental dyslexia. *Cerebral Cortex*, *28*(3), 963–973.

Wilson, A. A., & Chavez, K. J. (2014). *Reading and representing across the content areas: A classroom guide*. New York: Teachers College Press.

Witter, M. (2013). *Reading without limits: Teaching strategies to build independent reading for life*. San Francisco: Jossey-Bass.

Witzel, B., & Mize, M. (2018). Meeting the needs of students with dyslexia and dyscalculia. *SRATE Journal*, *27*(1), 31–39.

Wolf, M., & Gottwald, S. (2016). *Tales of literacy for the 21st century*. New York: Oxford University Press.

Wolf, M., Ullman-Shade, C., & Gottwald, S. (2016). Lessons from the reading brain for reading development and dyslexia. *Australian Journal of Learning Difficulties*, *21*(2), 143–156. https://doi.org/10.1080/19404158.2016.1337364

Wolfe, P. (2009). Brain Research and Education: Fad or foundation? *LOEX Conference Proceedings 2007*. Accessed at https://commons.emich.edu/loexconf2007/38 on June 23, 2023.

Yeatman, J. D., Dougherty, R. F., Ben-Shachar, M., & Wandell, B. A. (2012). Development of white matter and reading skills. *Proceedings of the National Academy of Sciences*, *109*(44), E3045–E3053. https://doi.org/10.1073/pnas.1206792109

Zheng, L., Chen, C., Liu, W., Long, Y., Zhao, H., Bai, X., Zhang, Z., Han, Z., Liu, L., Guo, T., Chen, B., Ding, G., & Lu, C. (2018). Enhancement of teaching outcome through neural prediction of the students' knowledge state. *Human Brain Mapping*, *39*(7), 3046–3057. https://doi.org/10.1002/hbm.24059

Zuk, J., Yu, X., Sanfilippo, J., Figuccio, M. J., Dunstan, J., Carruthers, C., Sideridis, G., et al. (2021). White matter in infancy is prospectively associated with language outcomes in kindergarten. *Developmental Cognitive Neuroscience*, *50*, Article 100973. https://doi.org/10.1016/j.dcn.2021.100973

INDEX

C

Calderón, M. E., 102
Castles, A., 5, 126
cause and effect, 53, 102, 104, 117–118
challenges in content-area reading, 98–99
Chavez, K., 109
Cheek, E. H. Jr., 100–102
clarification, 86
Clement, C., 128
cognitive overload, 113, 127
Cohen, J., 73
Cohen, L., 9
Cohen's *d*, 73
collocations, 40
compare and contrast, 53, 102–103, 117
comprehension, 4–6, 19, 21, 48–50,
    125, 129
        assessing, 66
        construction of understanding, 47–48
        defined, 47
        neuroplasticity, 10
        phonics and, 32
        reading development, 48–50
        strategies for teaching, 49–59
consolidation of neural networks, 10–30
consonant-vowel-consonant (CVC) words,
    28, 30–31, 35–37, 129
consonant-vowel-consonant words that end
    in *e* (CVCE words), 33
construction of understanding, 47–48
contextual vocabulary, 37–38
continuous vs. discontinuous letter
    sounds, 35
Cooperative Integrated Reading and
    Composition, 77
corrective feedback, 131
COVID-19 pandemic, 4
        effects on reading progress, 98–99

D

Daroczy, G., 3
data-based, collaborative decision–making,
    74–75, 79
de Blas, G. D., 3
de Bono, E., 106
decoding, 7, 28, 31, 34
        defined, 12
        neuroplasticity, 10
Dehaene, S., 9–10, 13
describe the noun, 43

description or attribution, 53, 102–103
descriptive text, 54, 116
development of speed and efficiency, 14–16
DIBELS screening tool, 66, 82–83, 88
Dieker, L., 119
differentiation, 74, 76, 79
digraphs, 35–36
direct instruction, 75
directive practice, 131
discipline-specific strategies, 110–111
        mathematics, 111–113
        science, 118–119
        social studies, 113–118
"doing history," 111
Dole, J. A., 125
Dolittle, F., 74
Dougherty, R., 15
Drop Everything and Read (DEAR), 44
during-the-reading strategies, 99
        questions, 101
Durkin, 47
dyslexia, 16–18
        defined, 16
        strong visual memories, 82

E

effect size, 72–73
effective programs to teach phonics, 36–37
effective sequence to teach letter sounds, 35
Elkonin boxes, 30
Elliott, Grigorenko, 64
Elliott, J., 18
essential principles for RTI practices
        data-based, collaborative decision–
            making, 74–75
        differentiation, 74, 76
        evidence-based classroom instruction,
            74–75
        evidence-based remedial supports,
            74, 77
        multi-tiered supports, 74, 77
        progress monitoring, 74, 76
        universal screening, 74
establishing learning goals, 85
evaluating and documenting, 89, 91–95
evidence-based classroom instruction, 66,
    74–75, 79
evidence-based practice, 1
        applied consistently, 5–6
evidence-based remedial supports, 74, 77, 79

Every Teacher Is a Literacy Teacher Series
Edited by Mark Onuscheck and Jeanne Spiller
Written by acclaimed experts and practitioners, the Every Teacher Is a
Literacy Teacher series details how to promote literacy growth across
disciplines and grade bands. Learn how to build a common language, work
in collaborative teams, implement literacy-infused instruction, and more.
BKF903, BKF910, BKF908, BKF915, BKF902, BKF901, BKF904, BKF907

Clearing the Path for Developing Learners
Peg Grafwallner
All learning is built on a foundation of essential literacy skills. With this
book, educators will gain the tools needed to apply these literacy skills
in every subject to support developing students in becoming better
readers, writers, thinkers, and speakers.
BKG105

Read Alouds for All Learners
Molly Ness
In *Read Alouds for All Learners: A Comprehensive Plan for Every
Subject, Every Day*, Grades PreK–8, Molly Ness provides a
compelling case for the integration, or reintegration, of the read
aloud in schools and a step-by-step resource for preK–8 educators
in classrooms.
BKG116

Teaching With Purpose
Karen Gazith
The most effective teachers are those who are both purposeful
and intentional in their daily work. Built on seven well-researched
principles, this resource outlines how new and veteran teachers can
thoughtfully cultivate a rich learning environment conducive to the
success of every student.
BKF974

a division of

Solution Tree | Press
Solution Tree

Visit SolutionTree.com or call 800.733.6786 to order.

Wait! Your professional development journey doesn't have to end with the last pages of this book.

We realize improving student learning doesn't happen overnight. And your school or district shouldn't be left to puzzle out all the details of this process alone.

No matter where you are on the journey, we're committed to helping you get to the next stage.

Take advantage of everything from **custom workshops** to **keynote presentations** and **interactive web and video conferencing**. We can even help you develop an action plan tailored to fit your specific needs.

Let's get the conversation started.

Call 888.763.9045 today.

SolutionTree.com